VISITATIONS
&CONVERSATIONS

Carole Bromley

Psychic Medium

Living Spirit Publishing

First published 2018

Dedicated to

My Mum, Dad and Sister in Heaven, to whom I love and thank for always being a part of my life, then and now

And, to my beautiful and inspirational Spirit Guides working with me at this present time, without you, I couldn't do this. You have given me many blessings. Thank You

Hannah, Nick, Paul, Janet, Che-Che, Cherokee

We're just having a conversation –

Like old times

You too?

I'm sorry for your loss

Table of Contents

Acknowledgments

Special thanks to my Hubby, Stephen Bromley, who is always there for me. And, whilst he may not understand this very special gift and spiritual passion I have, he has always supported me – once I told him I didn't need a strait jacket that is! He has kept me fed and watered over the last four years whilst writing this book, that's for sure. He has allowed me to open up our home without question to complete strangers. And, to people who come to see me in the hope of having a conversation with their visitors from the Other Side.

I also have to thank my crazy, but beautiful niece Beverley Latham for the love and support shown to me during the time it's taken in writing this book. Without you, I would have had to do all the housework! And without you, I wouldn't have anyone else in the family to pass this gift down to. I know you will make it just as special as I have, I'm so pleased to share it with you. Thank you.

I would also like to unequivocally thank my friends, Karon Campbell, Kay Haig and my school friend Lorraine Tierney for the special friendships, and love each of you have shown me throughout my spiritual journey. You have always endeavoured to be there for me. I owe you more than a cup of coffee!

I've been privileged to publish just a few of my client's *visitations and conversations* we have had. Without you, I wouldn't be able to share your cherished memories. I offer a huge amount of thanks to each and every one of you. Because of you, your loved one's memories can perhaps give hope to others. There are some visitations and conversations I have relived through my own memory that took place at some of my shows too. I have endeavoured to change the names of those who wished to remain anonymous for the sake of their family.

Naturally, I also offer thanks to the Professor's Ray J Paul and Professor Ian Angell for the advice and guidance given to me over the years. Thank you for your *visitations and conversations* that allowed me to work in 'natural' conditions, and with my 'own subjects' from the Spirit World. My friends are your friends.

I also thank Simone, my chosen editor who painstakingly worked with me to shape my manuscript. I did however dabble with a little bit of editing after, so any errors that are spotted I can own up as mine.

Last, but not least, my world would not be the same without our furry family; Missy, Mindy, Summer-Holly, Sexi-Lexi, the fish in the tank, minus the shark as he died last night. And to my lovely, strange but sweet street cats named Cheeky, and Doris who always come knocking on my door for a hug and a rug. They must also be the most well-fed street cats in the neighbourhood.

21ˢᵗ Century Medium

"Carole Bromley is a Psychic Medium, author of 'The Living Spirit, One Woman's Battle Amongst Ghosts, Spirits and The Living'. Carole is also a gifted 21st Century Medium who is highly acclaimed for her acute honesty in delivering accurate messages from the Spirit World. Her togetherness and partnership in working with Spirits is suffused with an unforced 'naturalness', showing us that our dear departed loved ones really are closer to us than we realise. Carole says that we all live in one world; she is completely at ease walking and working amongst them and sharing her experiences.

Following on from her success with personal and group readings, it was inevitable that Carole would move on to be successful in public demonstrations and public engagements. Carole has been developing on her two decades of experience in understanding the Spirit World, Spirit functioning, and Spiritual energy. That knowledge includes insights into scientific research and particularly how the scientific community relates and responds to psychic functioning. 'Carole is one of the most honest people I have ever met. She gives information that seems unnervingly accurate. I would recommend her'! How would I describe Carole? Totally without guile. A genuinely nice, decent person, who has a mission to help others, Carole has a wicked sense of humour, a self-deprecating style, and an empathy with her audiences that adds a light touch to her demonstrations, and this sets her apart". *Professor Ian Angell (London School of Economics)*

Joey Madia
Paranormal Investigator

A disclaimer to start. I am a paranormal researcher who is married to a psychic medium. My daughter is also a psychic medium. Given the sad fact that, in this day and age, a war is still being waged by many in the scientific community and other gatekeepers and cynics against giving any legitimacy to mediumship and investigative study of the paranormal, it may be easy for someone to simply say, as many do when I try to explain these things, that "You already believe, so you cannot be objective."

That statement makes no sense. I do, however, believe that there is life in some form after death. I also believe there are portals and multiple dimensions and sentient beings that vibrate at a higher level than living human beings and so do not behave according to traditional scientific laws. And I believe that an understanding of mediumship and what we call the paranormal is vital to the progression of the human race beyond its current and very limited way of living. A little research will show you that, for over 60 years, the United States, United Kingdom, and many other countries have poured hundreds of millions of dollars into the study and exploitation of these areas.

It is one thing to read a book, and another to experience the author at work. I was lucky enough some months ago to experience Bromley's way of working by observing a reading she did for my wife. Everything that she discusses in this book about her philosophy, her methods, and her unique, humor-filled approach to psychic mediumship was on display in the reading.

This is Bromley's second book about her life as a psychic medium. Not having read *The Living Spirit, One Woman's Battle Amongst Ghosts, Spirits and The Living* (2009), I am hazarding a guess here, but, judging from the title, it seems she has made the journey to more peace of mind and ease with her gifts since the publication of her first book. This is important, because skills such as Bromley's are not always appreciated by the majority of the public and the institutions that govern them.

Visitations & Conversations is, to my tastes—and in-line with a currently popular genre of nonfiction—a perfect blend of memoir and case studies/ testimonials. With her trademark sense of humor and colorful language, Carole shares her journey from childhood to now—with its many challenges, from financial struggles, to early family deaths, to health issues and the loss of a child of her own—all of which inform her relationship with the realm of the dead in profound ways.

As Bromley states in the opening pages, "I don't convince anyone to believe in life after death." This is an approach that I believe is invaluable if psychic mediumship and paranormal research are going to gain more credibility—and the deck is stacked against them for many reasons, including the rampant lies and exaggerations that are part and parcel of so-called Reality TV paranormal shows. My wife and I share Bromley's philosophy and approach. All one can do is be professional, share the messages received, and maintain peace of mind knowing you are helping people. The end-of-book testimonials would hopefully make any cynic see the value of the work she does.

That, to me, is the core of this book. Through her many case studies, including testimonials from clients, Bromley makes a strong case for how much psychic mediumship helps people make peace with the loss of loved ones, be it through infant deaths, suicides, illnesses, old age, or accidents. Human beings have mystified death to the point that it's a shadow cast over life. To know that there is life beyond death, that those we have lost are at peace, that they are watching over us, helping us, and helping each other, is a great gift.

Another aspect of Bromley's philosophy is that "there are no poltergeists or demons I write about." Entities that can be called demonic are truly few and far between. People often retain their personality after death—as I have seen through my firsthand experiences—and not all are pleasant. This is by and large what people are experiencing when they assume a "demonic" presence. It is an important distinction.

A prevalent aspect of Carole's journey is the obstacles she's faced from the establishment and her quest to earn respect. Her credentials are impressive: "I am a Psychic Medium, Reiki Teacher, Past Life Regressionist, Spiritual Teacher, Author, [and] Oracle Card Reader." She has been practicing her skills and developing her calling for more than 20 years. In any other field this would demand considerable respect. She also relates that she comes from a long line of people with psychic ability. This is the case with other mediums I know.

The final chapter is titled "Science v Psychic Functioning." It does not go into detail about how government-funded psychological-operations programs (such as those run during the Cold War by the Defense and Central Intelligence Agencies and Stanford Research Institute) spent hundreds of millions of dollars on the study of people like Bromley and my wife, but how governments don't spend that kind of money on programs like Remote Viewing without some foundational belief in the truth of psychic mediumship.

Bromley refers to herself as an "Ambassador" for the deceased, and, if that was a formal position, I would certainly nominate her. How she treats both sides of the veil with equal respect, how she feels a clear responsibility in working with and representing both worlds, and her embracing her role as intermediary and messenger even when it was difficult in her professional and personal life is inspiring.

If you know a medium, want to know more about mediumship, or have questions about life after death, this is an excellent resource. It is also a strong example of how a sense of humor enhances both the memoir and the memoirist's life and work.

Foreword
Second Time Around

Hello my darlings! It's only four years later, but it's here. Yay! My second book since writing '*The Living Spirit, One Woman's Battle Amongst Ghosts, Spirits and the Living*' way back in 2009.

For those who have waited in anticipation of this publication, I do apologise. I'm a one-man band, so to speak. My working role as a Psychic Medium, wife and mother to three dogs, one cat, two street cats, a few fish and many fundraisers has kept me busy. But, I really hope you enjoy this second part of my journey.

I have to tell you how honoured and blessed I am to bring more people into this part of my story. I'm sharing their memories of laughter and tears through the countless *visitations and conversations* we've had between both worlds. I'm bringing you real-life events and dramas that I face as a Psychic Medium, including the continued battles with 'Absent Ghosts, Spirits and The Living'. I reference a little bit about religious and scientific views, too. And, if you think you were going crazy through what you think you see or hear, calm down. I'm going to be sharing stories with you that will put things back into perspective.

Best of all, I bring you evidence through the messages of *visitations and conversations* I've given and received from Spirit souls, themselves. Memories referenced that are a continuum of survival in an afterlife. However, I'm not the one who is going to tell you there is no such thing as death. The people I read for, they are the ones who will tell you how they, too, believe in the Soul's survival. They will tell you how their own evidence, through my conversations with them and their deceased loved ones, has been absolutely nothing more than absolute evidence.

I don't convince anyone to believe in life after death. That is something you, my reader, will have to decide for yourself. But, not through anything written here. You will only believe what you know is true through your own spiritual experience. All I am doing here is telling you how it is and how it isn't.

Before purchasing this book and to avoid disappointment, there are no poltergeists or demons written about here. What you will find within is all set out in the contents – a story of me, a Psychic Medium, helping to heal people, their family, and their friends in both worlds.

Lastly, you need to know I'm not very good with words, I'm being honest. So, I hope I have done enough to demonstrate my life and the life of those who have got on my nerves. What matters most is I hope I have done enough for those who have loved and lost. I hope I've done enough for the Spirit souls who keep me employed. Thank you for being part of my amazing journey. God Bless you.

Chapter 1
A Different World

I see Spirits, I hear Spirits, I talk to dead people. I have sensed their presence since childhood. Scientists have told people like me with psychic functioning that we are mistaken. I am mistaken. But, what do they know? They haven't shared my experiences. How could they possibly know what it is to be a Psychic, or even a Medium?

Some people will retain their psychic intuition and use it. However, for most, social pressures will suppress it to a greater or lesser extent. We will all have, and share experiences connected to those moments of 'knowing' or 'happening' of something - despite it seeming quite illogical. Here's something worth mentioning: Mediums take the development of these abilities much further to include advanced psychic functioning.

I have been blessed to give thousands of inspirational messages from the many Spirit souls of friends and relatives who have come to see me. Spirit souls all wanting to tell their way of life in the Heavenly realms. I want to share my experiences and my life as a Psychic Medium with you. I want you to wear my shoes as you walk with me in this continued spiritual part of my journey. All I ask is that you keep your heart and your mind open in the same way I have, because this is what allows the love and memories in both worlds to be made possible.

As a Medium, I will share not just the voices of those who come to seek messages from loved ones - but share the voices of Spirit souls themselves. They are the ones who truly need an Ambassador to speak on their behalf. I can, and I do speak on their behalf. I am blessed to be their Ambassador.

Throughout this journey - I will open and close the door to Heaven. I will give you a glimpse of this incredible and amazing world we are all part of and share on a daily basis. Whether you know it or not. Join me as you read about and listen to some of the many affluent voices from the Spirit World. Learn about what it's like being a Medium in my world with people who have loved and lost family and friends to the Heavenly Realms.

There are battles I have met through my belief system - through those whose views are different from my own. These are the experiences I hope to bring to you, as well as a better awareness and understanding of the battles I, and many others like me encounter.

I have already described the beginnings of my Spiritual journey in my first book: '*The Living Spirit: One Woman's Battle Amongst Ghosts, Spirits and The Living*'. I hope you will continue to also enjoy this, the second book of my *Visitations and Conversations* with Spirit souls who have moved me along, inspired me and allowed me to grow with them. I hope you will enjoy their messages of their memories they have shared with their family and friends.

All I ask is that you allow yourself to be part of this beautiful alliance the Spirit World and I share. A world that has been life-changing for souls, living and dead, in both worlds. Perhaps made changes in your own world too. Allow yourself to become embraced in a beautiful, vibrant and very beautiful world place one day will be yours. That much I can promise you.

19

Chapter 2
Disembodied Voices

Welcome to my world - a world that we all inhabit, but one the majority of humanity denies. A world where we can question our own sanity when hearing disembodied (Spirits of dead people) voices talking to us, but no one is there, or are they? Only you can know the answer to that question.

Whether we like it or not, we are all going to join those who have gone before us to that beautiful place we call Heaven. The Spirit World. We will all continue to co-exist in the afterlife as a wonderful spark of love surrounded by a divine light. We will all exist in a life after death that is the survival of our consciousness. A life where we exist as a Spirit soul. We will all, upon disengaging from our physical body, connect beautifully to the God source and everything that is divine and of love. We will all be loved and feel loved.

I was born in Tyldesley, Manchester, England, Dad's place of birth. I lived there with my parents, two older brothers, older sister and twin brother. That was at least until we relocated to Mum's birthplace on the outskirts of London, in Yiewsley, Middlesex, when I was eight years old. My memory of Tyldesley was that of a small town where everyone knew one another. Our house backed onto huge fields and a farm. Mum would often send me off to the farm shop to buy a few potatoes, vegetables or fresh eggs. I was quite tiny as a child so couldn't carry much, but I'd hop, skip and jump as I made my way there and back in the short time it took. I would watch the cows grazing in the field as I passed them by. I would also have a name for each of them, too. Only, I'd mostly always forget what I' named them so would call them all 'Billy' anyway.

Tyldesley was a coal mining town and Dad, himself, had done some time down the pits before working at the foundries. There would always be piles of coal in a street close by, so it was normal for me and the other kids of the neighbourhood to have fun playing on them. It was normal for kids to get dirty and covered in coal from head to toe. Spending time sitting in a tin bath in front of a coal fire was also a normal way of life.

Our entertainment as kids would be to chalk numbers in squares on the pavement with chards of coal. We'd kick a tin of old boot polish around on the squares as we played hopscotch for hours on end. At night, many of us would be out in the street tagging onto each other, laughing cheerily as we chugged up and down in the middle of the road pretending to be a ghost train. Our parents would be standing at the garden gates - or sitting on each other's garden wall chatting to one another as they watched over us.

I would also spend many hours playing with my dolls. Every Friday, Mum used to buy me a doll from the local market. I got to have quite a collection. Strangely enough, the dolls somehow became part of my 'other world.' I also found the more I played with the dolls, the more I would hear the voices. Call me crazy, but my dolls and I had real conversations. The dolls were crazy, not me, at least that's what I used to think!

I also used to think talking dolls only existed in my world until I saw a Ventriloquist. I was six years old watching a man stood in front of me with a giant-sized puppet doll sitting on his lap. I was in the classroom at infant school and everyone was laughing at him. Everyone except me. I didn't laugh because I didn't think he was funny. I thought quite the opposite.

It scared me how this man could talk to his doll, and his doll talked back to him. Just like my dolls did with me. I wet myself on the spot where I was standing. I was terrified. Everyone in the class was looking at me, looking at the puddle of pee I was standing in. I remember how the teacher rushcd me outside the classroom trying to calm me down as I screamed. Mum had to come and collect me. Even to this day, Ventriloquists freak me out, and I still can't bring myself to watch them.

I have come a long way since talking to dolls and having nonsensical conversations with them. Now my conversations are shared between the living and the dead, in both worlds. I guess my conversations in 'Dolly World' kick-started my career as a Medium. It was also when I gained my ability in Clairaudience (clear hearing), and to some extent, Clairvoyance (clear seeing).

Looking back, I recall my very first Spirit manifestation, at just six years old - a time when I was first awakened with this 'other world'. It was when Mum had kept me off school because I was ill. Of course, my Mum was no different to other Mums, who would make a fuss every time there was something wrong. She would have me dragged off down to the doctor's to be checked over. If she didn't, she wouldn't stop worrying and think I'd got something terribly wrong with me. Worse still, thought I was dying.

On this one particular day, there was a storm thrashing around outside, and Mum didn't take me to the doctor. Instead, she laid me on the sofa, and told me to rest as she covered me with a blanket. Only I couldn't rest. The storm and my fear of it got the better of me. I stood up on the sofa to look out the window, watching the lightening flash across the sky. I was bawling my eyes out because the storm terrified me, but there was something else that was odd that attracted my attention. Standing in front of our house was a clown who was looking straight at me. He looked silly as he danced in the middle of the road in the pouring rain.

I had no idea where the clown went, but he disappeared. I didn't even know how he disappeared, he just did. Then, out of nowhere, the clown walked through our living room wall and to where I was standing on the sofa. I was still bawling my eyes out. He was happy and jolly, but he didn't cheer me up. Turning to leave, he made his exit so effortlessly back through the wall he had come through. He was laughing and waving at me as he disappeared.

This clown taught me my first valuable lesson: humans cannot walk through walls, only Spirits can! Our energy is not as tangible as theirs. It was certainly one of those 'do not try this at home' moments when I had tried to follow the clown through the wall. He laughed, I cried. My piercing scream brought Mum running to my rescue and tending to the bump that had formed on my forehead. I hated that clown.

I would feel quite comfortable having conversations with disembodied voices as a kid during the day. The voices would never bother me with all their chatter. It was at night that I didn't like them talking. I was quite the drama queen when it came to bedtime. I would pretend to Mum that I wasn't tired, just so I wouldn't be left to sleep in a room that whispered to me. When bedtime came, you could hear her shout, "Come on Carole, bed." She would call my twin brother, too. We'd both be marched up the stairs with Mum following behind us.

After being tucked into bed with a kiss on the cheek, Mum would go back downstairs. I'd jump right up and run after her, telling her that she had to come up to bed and stay with me. The voices came to bed with me. I was a nightmare. The voices were a nightmare. Mum would say, "There's nobody there!" when I knew there was. There was always someone there.

I'd have to have Mum do a regular ritual check of my bedroom before I got into bed. I'd have to be satisfied no one was hiding behind the door or in the cupboards. I was afraid someone might reach out and grab me, either when Mum left the room, or worse still, when I was sleeping. With so many pervasive voices, it was only natural for me to ask Mum to do a quick field observation.

Don't get me wrong, I wasn't possessed or obsessed, it was just something I needed to know, and something I needed Mum to do. I needed to know I could sleep well. We all need to know there's no one lurking around our room when we go to sleep. We all need a good night's sleep once the lights are turned off. We don't need ghosts or dead people hanging out in our cupboards, or standing at the bottom of our bed when the lights go out, right?

I didn't know the voices I heard were coming from dead people. I was a kid. People didn't talk about the dead or how they could talk to you, nor anything else they could do. I was ill-educated on dead people because it was something not openly spoken about back then. I always felt alone growing up with the disembodied voices. Truth is, I was alone.

Even though I loved living in my childhood home there came a time when we had to leave. Mum wanted to be with the rest of her family and so we moved. I was eight years old when we moved from Manchester to London and into my Nan and Granddad's house. It was overcrowded with the seven of us, but we managed. Besides, we didn't have to live there long before Mum and Dad bought a house in Edgar Road, Yiewsley. It was a lovely semi-detached house which was only a few streets away from Nan and Granddads, which was good, as we could walk the five minutes it took. We could visit our Grandparents whenever we wanted.

Yet, it didn't matter where we moved to, though, as the voices always moved with us – moved with me. I relive some of those memories in my first book, '*The Living Spirit' One Woman's Battle Amongst Ghosts, Spirits and The Living.*"

It was probably less than two years since moving into our new home when Mum and Dad started arguing. Those arguments caused them to separate and our family to split up. Once again, we had to move. Dad found a room to rent somewhere. One of my brothers had left home already so he wouldn't be moving with us. My other brother and sister stayed somewhere else. Quite where they stayed, I never knew. I always assumed they went back to our Grandparent's house.

After the house was sold, we were considered homeless. The Council placed me, Mum and my twin brother into sheltered housing over at High Grove House in Ruislip, another town on the outskirts of London. I hated the sheltered housing, as even though we had a roof over our heads, we weren't together as a family.

High Grove House was a huge mansion. It was dark and dreary. I hated walking down the pitch black and sombre tree lined driveway to reach the front door. The only lights we could see were those coming from inside the house. When you entered the mansion, you would be met with a very cold, old and wide staircase leading up to the huge landing. There was no carpet that would help to keep the building warm. Instead, linoleum covered the floors, including the staircase. The ceilings were very high which would give an echo effect when you spoke. Coming off from the landing were other rooms which were occupied by single women and their children. We also had to spend a Christmas in this gloomy looking place.

The room we lived in was drab, dismal and with walls painted orange. The ceiling was high and seemed to make the room feel huge. We had one bed which my twin brother and I shared with Mum. That winter was freezing cold. Ice would cover the window panes adjacent to our bed. Our room had no radiators; instead Mum would have to light a fire. It would be so cold we could see our breath as we spoke. We would pull up chairs to the glowing warm fire and the red-hot coals to keep warm, and I always went to bed wearing flannelette pyjamas and my woolly mittens.

We ate cornflakes for breakfast and often again for dinner. I remember how Mum would keep a pint of bottled milk, along with other food and drink in the cupboard in our room. She didn't like going into the shared kitchen along the corridor to store stuff in the fridge, as people would more often than not nick it. I remember too a time when I took a bottle of milk from the cupboard. I had taken a sip and spat it out on the floor in disgust. It had gone off. I never drank milk on its own after that - once was quite enough.

Mum being Mum would always make sure we got up early enough to get washed and dressed. She never ever wanted us to be late to catch the train for school. Even throughout the freezing cold dark winter nights and mornings and the snow storms of the 1970s, Mum got us to school on time. Our attendance at school never suffered. She always made sure we were always clean and tidy. Besides being a single parent, Mum was also a very proud woman. There was simply no way she would have people talk about her kids looking dirty or wearing dirty clothes. Even though most of our clothes were second-hand we still always looked clean and tidy. That alone was something for Mum to be proud of.

We all thought we had fallen on our feet having waited a good part of a year to move out of High Grove. The Council relocated us to a new home in Austin Waye, Uxbridge, Middlesex. The house was so small, but we were happy we could live as a family once again. The bath dominated one corner of the kitchen. A sink and drainer adjacent to it. There was no indoor toilet, only a small brick outhouse in the garden. The small living room is where we watched pay-as-you-go television and ate meals on our laps. The upstairs had three bedrooms. My two older brothers in one room at the front, with my sister in the small box room at the back. Me, mum and my twin brother squeezed into one bed in the other back room. Because there was no indoor loo, a bucket would be in the corner at the top of the stairs in case we needed it in the night. There was always a need for the bucket. One good thing to note about the house was having a nice long garden which backed onto a playing field.

It was a really good feeling to be in this house and having the family all together. Unfortunately, that was a feeling short lived. It wasn't long after leaving Highgrove House and moving into our new home that Christine and her fiancé died in a fatal car crash. New Year's Eve, 1970. My sister, just eighteen years old, had become engaged to her boyfriend, Colin. I was happy, we were all happy, especially since my parents had gone through a nasty separation and awaiting a divorce.

Since everyone in our house was going out to celebrate and welcome in the New Year, Mum had arranged for a neighbour to pop in and keep an eye on me and my twin brother. We would be okay staying in to watch the telly. No one knew how it would turn into a night we would never forget. No one except me, that is.

Standing in the living room, I was startled when I heard a voice that seemed to come from next to me, yet no one was there. The voice said, "Say goodbye to your sister she's not coming back." I ignored the voice believing it to be my imagination. The voice repeated the words again, "Say goodbye to your sister, you won't see her again." Something wasn't right, mostly because I felt uneasy. I felt uncomfortable. The voice that spoke to me was not a whisper, neither was it distorted in sound. It was as clear as a whistle.

I hated the voices and wanted nothing more to do with them after my sister and her fiancé had died. The car they were travelling in with friends had skidded on black ice, rolled over and hit a tree, killing them both instantly. Besides the weather, the driver of the car was also drunk. New Year's Eve would never be the same again, ever. The voices went away, temporarily.

I blamed myself for that ghostly voice, I thought it was me thinking horrible thoughts, when it wasn't. The thoughts and the voices were not of my making, and I never told anyone about the voices or what I heard. I didn't say anything because I was scared. I was scared I would be blamed for the tragedy and what happened. The voices seemed to go away for a while.

After losing Christine, Mum's heart remained broken. Yet, she carried on when she could easily have given up. Mum was a beacon of her own light, who as a single parent cared for and looked after her five kids. To live through times like we had does give you an extraordinary sense of determination to make life count, no matter how much or how little you have. We really didn't have much, but the amount of love our Mum had for her kids and family was everything.

I accepted my sister's death and the voices that had haunted me for so long when I started to research the paranormal. I researched what I could about those with psychic functioning. I was probably in my forties when I started on a personal mission to find answers. In truth, I never stopped looking for answers, yet, I couldn't live life blaming myself for something I wasn't responsible for. I couldn't blame myself for my sister's death, something I had done for so many years.

Yet, disembodied voices are quite a common phenomenon with millions of people who claim to hear them. I'm no different, although, it was a big change when I went from hearing voices to seeing Spirit manifest in front of me. I was unprepared for the change and didn't like it. But, it wasn't just the voices that I had to live with. It was other stuff too. Stuff you will read about in this book. I also found the older I got the more *unexplained* experiences I would have. Those experiences taught me what I needed to do and work at in order to evolve in this work.

Those experiences gave me a lot to deal with. I just didn't know how. For instance, there were times when dead people would pop-up right in front of me, anywhere and everywhere. I'd be eating dinner with Hubby at the table when I'd see 'others' sitting with us. I'd perhaps be talking to someone and feel someone else's eyes looking through mine and staring at the person I was talking to. I'd begin to see or hear things connected to that person. I'd also see reflections of ghostly faces appear in the bathroom mirror on numerous occasions, including the time when my deceased sister's face appeared. Dead people also kept appearing at my bedside in the middle of the night. Call me crazy, but I'm pretty sure that word got out amongst the dead 'Soul parties' were held nightly at my house!

Naturally, there were times during the night I would be petrified and tell whoever showed themselves at my bedside to "Fuck off!" That was back then, though, when dead people started appearing in front of me, frightening the living daylights out of me. And, I certainly didn't invite them. Well, not intentionally. Of course, it goes without saying how I always used to have this feeling that someone was watching me, and of course it would be true, which was a little bit unnerving at times - well, quite a lot actually.

It wasn't until Hannah, my Spirit Guide, who came and introduced herself to me in a dream, told me how I shouldn't dismiss Spirit (dead people) because they come for a reason. She told me how I shouldn't dismiss dead people when they visit because they could be someone's loved one. She had a point, even though it wasn't a comfortable one. I came to grips with myself after that. I realised how I wouldn't like anyone talking to my sister in the way I had been speaking to those who visited me.

Thankfully, and please don't laugh because I know you may find it a little amusing, but I came to learn how my house wasn't the only house dead people hung out in. I often saw dead people in other people's houses, too, only they didn't know they were there. People don't always realise how the dead share their home with them. And I don't always like to tell them. Mostly because I know they wouldn't want to know.

People will often experience their own evidence of a visitation from a deceased soul, or something paranormal. For some, seeing a ghostly figure or hearing unexplained voices and noises can often cause a person to question their sanity. I know how many times I questioned my own. But, look at it this way, when a deceased person you know pays you a visit and you can see them, think of it as that soul sharing their love with you. Think of the experience as a special 'gift' you were given in seeing that person at the time of their visitation. Think of it as a blessing – because that's what it is. As I said, we can all hear voices or experience something paranormal. Some of us will acknowledge these experiences, whilst others will dismiss them.

An experience I wanted to embrace was doing shows where I could demonstrate evidence of an afterlife. I have done and continue to do many shows up and down the country. I remember one where there was a gentleman who certainly got to have his own disembodied experience. I was demonstrating in High Wycombe, England. It was the very first time for me in that venue. However, this man's experience happened just as I had announced a break after the first half. I turned to place the microphone on the speaker behind me when I heard a voice call out, "Carole." I swung around to acknowledge the person wanting to speak to me, but no one was there.

People in the hall were getting up and heading towards the door and bar for refreshments, and their own taste of 'Spirit.' I was puzzled as to who had called my name. I looked at the man sitting with a few ladies in the front row and asked, "Did you call me, darling?" He looked at me with a smile on his face as he replied, "No, not me, but I definitely heard someone call your name at the same time you did." I smiled at him, thinking he, too, knew he had heard a voice belonging to Spirit. I now know his name is Danny, I want to say Danny if you're reading this … it wasn't your imagination, but you knew that already!

I could feel so much Spiritual energy in the hall I was buzzing. People were buzzing. I was so proud of the conversations going on between both worlds. People were happy at being reunited with someone they love. They felt the love that was being shared, even if they weren't getting a message themselves, they were still very much part of sharing the love between both worlds.

When everyone returned and was seated for the second half of the show, I picked up the microphone asking, "Did anyone come up to me who wanted to speak to me before the break, please." No one answered. I asked again, "Okay, did any of you call my name, or call out the name, 'Carole' before you left the hall please?" But again, no one responded, no one put their hand up. I asked, "Is anyone else here called 'Carole?' No one responded, no one shared the same name as me.

People were looking at me as though I was mad. I didn't worry because it's a look I often get. However, I did owe my audience a brief explanation, so I mentioned having heard my name being called. I told my audience how the man sitting in the front row had heard my name being called, too, yet no one was there. He certainly knew what he had heard, and he looked pleased with himself. It's not like he heard disembodied voices every day - because it was something he probably wouldn't.

I give credit to Spirits who have taught me the way of their world. It's a world progressing, growing, interacting and sharing intelligent information with us. Nonetheless, being brought up in a world that consisted of disembodied voices was, I have come to learn, no coincidence. They, Spirit, knew what they were doing and why. Call me 'Cupid' but matchmaking and bringing souls together has turned out to be a job with many benefits – where both worlds can benefit.

I have learned how my development over the years has brought many rewards in helping people reunite with their loved ones in Heaven. It truly has been a life-changing experience for every departed loved one I have ever reunited to their family or friend. That is the work I do.

It's because of my sister, Christine, I am able to do this work. It's because of her I want to do this work. It is her who has taught me from the Spirit World how to appreciate my work. I thank her for sharing her knowledge that has allowed me to realise how precious life is in both worlds. Everything I do for deceased souls is incredibly important. My sister's own passing has helped me to understand the comfort I can bring when I reunite families and friends in both worlds. I know through the evidence deceased souls give me this certainty: 'no one's gone forever, but everyone lives forever!'

Since my sister passed, I know what it is to miss someone you love but can no longer hug. My sister and I have had to grow up with one another in different worlds. She has helped me unequivocally to understand about her world, the Spirit World, and how much it should mean to us all. Our conversations are never limited. She is, and always will be my very much missed BIG sister. We should have spent our lives growing up with one another, but instead, we have both learned to accept growing up together in each other's worlds. My sister has made me feel comfortable in sharing part of her world. She has always shared her world with me. That's what sisters do, they share. I don't care, I'm having the best of both worlds. I'm not crazy.

After all these years, I even share my sister's best friend, Elaine, with her. She lives around the corner from me and two doors up from where we used to live in Edgar Road; our first home after moving out of Nan and Granddad's. It was here she would hang out and go to school with my sister. Whenever I bumped into Elaine in town, I would have a little giggle with her. She would recall how I would get all bossy and tell her not to sit down in a particular chair. She thought I was well weird!

Whenever and wherever I played, my chairs were always occupied, apparently by dead people only I could see. Elaine told me how she would be fascinated as she watched how I would engage in strange conversations with myself. But, of course, I wouldn't be talking to myself. My friends were just different to my sister's. And, Christine, she knew I wasn't alone. She knew I had other 'friends.'

As the years went by the disembodied voices became more frequent and prominent. I would often find myself dismissing or ignoring them. I found them to be quite a distraction, if not irritating. They were invading my world with their frequent chatter. In my world, I would often hear lots of voices talking over one another, not making any sense. You know that feeling when you're in a really busy pub and hearing lots of voices from people speaking. Yet, no matter how loud the voices were, you can never make out who was saying what, no matter how far you stretched your ears. That's what's it's like for me with Spirit.

I came to learn and understand that I could not ignore the voice of Spirit when they spoke to me, especially if they wanted me to hear what they had to say. And, as much as I tried to ignore them, sometimes it was almost impossible.

I only stopped listening to the voices after my sister died. I shut them out completely. However, I felt compelled to take an interest in the disembodied voices that had become omnipresent once again and on their own accord. I was in my forties, perhaps before, it's hard to say when something has been with you for so long - you just get used to the normality of it. Nonetheless, I gradually became aware the voices were back.

I started to pay more attention, mostly because I was randomly hearing and experiencing things I couldn't explain. I began to know things about people that would come true. I would see into the future. I would see dead people at my bedside and in my house. I would be looking at a sea of dead people whenever I went into shops too. I would hear voices talking to me, talking to their loved ones who were walking with them around the aisles.

I didn't tell Hubby at first because I wasn't sure what was happening. I didn't want to bother him unnecessarily. I was scared what he might say. I was scared he would think I was some sort of lunatic. Which he did at one point!

I wasn't scared of the voices, but I did want to know more. The voices had my attention. It was a new awakening for me. Over the years I began to understand how the voices were a continuation of another part of my Spiritual journey. I was determined to learn and become a student and serve an apprenticeship to GOD and the Spirit World. I needed to gain further knowledge about Spiritual phenomena and sought to educate myself through research. I surfed the internet and read up on scientific experiments conducted on those with psychic functioning. I literally looked at everything

I could in order to make sense of anything that had to do with communications and the afterlife.

I needed answers, that much I did know. I couldn't live life feeling guilty in knowing I didn't do anything for my sister to prevent her death. I deserved to know how I was able to hear what I had heard on the night of her death. I wanted an explanation. I couldn't find one.

In the house I live now, and have lived in for over forty years, I went through a time where it wasn't my own. It was occupied – by dead people. I had reignited a link to the Spirit World through the readings online and in person that I was doing. Spirit knew I was interested.

But, in this same house, I also remember how I would push Hubby into a room because I was too afraid to go in it alone. Not that he noticed I pushed him. I really was scared to go in rooms in our house on my own. I was scared to be in my own home because of Spirit. You'd have to read my first book 'The Living Spirit: One Woman's Battle Amongst Ghosts, Spirits & The Living' to find out more.

Growing up, I never heard anyone openly talk about the dead or dead people. In retrospect, I didn't know any different either. Perhaps I wasn't the only one who hid it from their parents. Perhaps I wasn't the only one who was alone with visitors from the Other Side. I understand how parents in those days back then, during the 50's and 60's, perhaps the 70's and 80's too, often claimed children who talked to themselves, had 'imaginary friends'. Anything associated with ghostly, paranormal or spiritual experiences was not normal. It wasn't something people easily accepted in the way they do today.

If I'd have known at such a young age that the voices talking to me were coming from dead people, I just may not have been so willing to listen to them, or to play along with them as much as I had. Today, children are now being taken notice of more seriously. Children today talk about seeing Grandparents, even when they didn't know, or hadn't met them. It's not unusual for children to talk about, or to give an accurate description of a person who has visited them from Heaven. Some visitations may not be family, and the descriptions may not be of a Grandparent, or any relative connected to the family - in which case it's most likely to be ... someone else!

Thankfully, today, we have a clearer understanding of the paranormal, including Ghosts, Spirits, Psychics and Mediums, thanks to the media and the World Wide Web - information is freely available. Because of this, more people are talking about and sharing their paranormal experiences. People no longer feel a stigma in talking about ghosts, *visitations and conversations*, disembodied voices, or a psychic experience they've had.

It seems people are happy to keep their deceased loved one's memory alive even more so today. I know how talking about deceased loved ones can be really comforting as well as healing. I only wished my own mother, when she was alive, could have talked about Christine more. If she had, I know how it could have brought her the healing she needed. Sadly, mum actually hated talking about Christine and the loss of her child; it was too painful for her. I know she cried every day of her life until the day she died. I saw her tears, I felt her sadness. I also know how difficult it was for Mum in my being the spitting image of Christine. I was a constant reminder of the daughter she lost. Yet, it didn't stop her, or other people from calling me 'Christine.'

My mother was quite psychic herself, albeit a non-responsive psychic (a person who knows they are psychic, or sensitive to Spirit, but chooses not to acknowledge it). I believed this because as I grew up our thoughts and actions were very much in sync, and probably one reason we clashed with each other on numerous occasions.

It was always very difficult for my Mum to talk of the dead. This was a stance she continued throughout her life. I always felt because she didn't come to terms with losing her daughter, it was hard for her to talk about other *dead* people. I would see how anxious it made her when someone mentioned a person known to her had died.

Besides me and Mum having psychic abilities, which of course she wouldn't admit to, I have been told how my Nan, great Grandmother and great Grandfather were psychic. There is a lovely lady I know, now in her nineties, who told me how I have inherited my great Grandfather's abilities. My great Grandfather was apparently a Romany Gypsy. He would often wear a gold ear ring in each ear. I'm sad I never got to meet him, I'm sure he was quite a character. Apart from my niece Bev who is developing mediumship, and my great niece Gemma, who is learning tarot cards, there are no other family members who use their psychic abilities and this gift. For now, at least.

The Spirit World and our world is everything a training platform should be. It is Heaven's Open University with a multitude of modules to learn. Everyone graduates, in both worlds. No one ever fails because everyone in Heaven wants to help us. The least we can do is to help them, too.

Chapter 3
Psychic Intuition

Now, we move onto psychic functioning – but, first of all, let me tell you, I have no idea of the science behind this type of phenomena. All I know is that it is a natural and intelligent phenomenon which accounts for only one part of our brain. It is this small part of the brain located on the right-hand side of our head that allows us access to our sixth sense and psychic abilities. Our brain is a huge part of us that determines the multi-functional abilities used by each and every one of us on a daily basis. This sixth sense is activated by being aware of it, and how you can use it.

Psychic functioning actually starts as soon as a foetus begins to develop and grow inside its mother's womb. It is this beginning whereby the unborn will use its sixth sense ability as probably the most important sense of them all. This sense will help an unborn child to adequately communicate and feel protected throughout its growth, and beyond.

Between a Mother and her unborn, this psychic sense is a really important ability that can be used to telepathically communicate feelings and emotions from inside the womb. So, if the mother is stressed, this can have the same reflection on the baby. Inside the womb, the unborn can also use its sixth sense to be aware of danger when the mother is under threat. This ability is signalled by the mother to the baby's brain – very much in a way that the unborn can connect to this signal and sense the feeling of danger, themselves. Every new-born baby has the ability to use psychic functioning.

Even though I've had a psychic ability since childhood, it doesn't always work. And it can't always be used on tap. There have been countless times whereby people have put me on the spot and almost forced me to use psychic functioning to answer their questions. I only wished I could have answered some of my own questions as a psychic. That, in itself, could be described as a good use of my psychic senses and psychic energy.

Since each of us is psychic, we can have an ability of using our psychic senses without realising it. I know I've spoken to countless people who have experienced using their psychic sense with or without their own awareness. Especially when it comes to sensing death.

Sensing death is something many of us seem to be able to connect to when the time comes. So, it's not unusual to have a feeling of 'knowing' when someone has died - that is your psychic sense working. Some people also have a feeling and a 'knowing' when someone *is* going to die. They know because their own chilling psychic sense and prediction comes true.

This feeling of having a psychic 'knowing' is especially true when visiting someone who is dying. For instance, look at how just the thought of leaving a loved one in hospital, hospice or at home can be quite a worry for some. The predicament whether to step out for a coffee, a puff on a cigarette, or nip home to shower and change can be one of the hardest decisions a person can make.

The worry about whether a loved one will be alive or not when returning from stepping out can be a heavy burden. Many of us have been in that situation whereby if we do step out, we may return to find our loved one has already died. Yet, you just 'knew' something would happen during your absence. Your gut instinct and sixth sense told you something was going to happen, but you convinced yourself nothing would until you got back. It happens. And the kiss you popped on your loved one's forehead before you stepped out, you knew it would be your last kiss.

Yet, everything happens for a reason. If you have stepped out and not made it back in time for those last moments, there was a reason you weren't meant to. No matter how hard or how deep you search in your heart - that reason why you chose to leave at that precise time may never come. It's far better, instead, to accept how it was just meant to be that way. On the other hand, it may be that you do get to be with your loved one during their dying moments. It may be that you did get to see someone you love hanging on for you to arrive before they died. We don't always get it right because fate is not always in our hands.

There are other ways our psychic senses work with us which can easily be over-looked or dismissed when something happens. Receiving a text message, phone call, email, or visit from a person we are thinking of at that very moment is no coincidence. We have a direct telephone line linking our thoughts across the universe to those who are on our mind. That is also including those in the Spirit World, too. The results of our psychic intuition and thoughts always speak for themselves.

Yet, as lovely as it all sounds, there are times when I see things I'd rather not see. For instance, I may see a miscarriage with a pregnancy. Yet, I can't tell a mother she will lose her baby. God, no, I couldn't. Sadly, not all pregnancy predictions are healthy ones either. I can't always see if the baby will grow full term, nor if the baby will be born with or without any complications. Perhaps because I'm not meant to know, I don't know.

Further predictions I may also see are when a client may break up with their partner. It's hard. I would tell the truth in what I see. Usually, what I see is what is already known anyway by a client. Particularly if their partner is having an affair. All I am doing is putting a more positive outlook on the relationship. When one door closes another one always opens. Besides, as with all relationship questions, I always tell the client asking it's not for me or Spirit to make or break relationships. Matters of the heart must come from the heart.

I'm not going to be able to do anything about the negatives I see. There are things I simply cannot control. There are things I simply cannot change. Whatever happens, happens. What will be, will be. Change is either made by us, or for us.

Change is actually something people look for when they come to me for a reading. I can usually see what influences and energies are manifesting by use of my sixth (psychic) sense or by using Oracle (Tarot) cards. I have been reading Tarot successfully over two decades now. When I see into the future during a reading, it can go two ways: either the information is positive and welcomed, or not liked and dismissed. I can get told I'm wrong. I don't mind being told I'm wrong when the person I'm reading for doesn't think my prediction is accurate. I frequently hear how I got it right, which is always encouraging. My track record is beyond good. Whilst I may not be able to change the world of the people who come to see me, I can give something positive to endorse change in that person's world. Anything that is healing has a place in everyone's personal and universal journey.

Sometimes, people like to be prepared for the future. And, in my experience there are times when my predictions can be welcomed. Like the time when I was reading for Kathleen, a client of mine on Skype. I found myself congratulating her on her pregnancy. To my surprise, but probably more to hers, she told me she wasn't pregnant. I explained to her how I saw her stomach getting bigger, which is my sign for being pregnant. The very next day Kathleen sent me a message telling me she had done a pregnancy test. The test had confirmed she was indeed pregnant. Fortunately, she was also very happy at the news. Both her and her partner couldn't wait to be parents again. They had a lot of planning to do for a future they had no idea existed until I told them. I love being the bearer of good news, especially when it's 'Baby' news!

News of pregnancies and dates of births is not uncommon for me to accurately predict during a reading. I have given countless predictions which have been verified true and correct by new Mummies. A friend of mine and mummy-to-be, Dominique, told me how I predicted her baby would be born on the 11th of the month. Noah came along on the 11th as I predicted. I also told her the number seven would be significant and it was, as Noah weighed in at 7lb 3oz.

Another client, Sam, sent me a message to tell me how I predicted the number 8 during her reading, which would prove to be very significant and important. Sam confirmed how she went into labour when her water broke at 8 o'clock. In addition to that, baby Ronnie was delivered happy and healthy in a room with the number 8 on the door. There have been many more accurate pregnancy predictions, but too many to mention.

My psychic ability and seeing into the future are not a claim I take lightly, but one that I have demonstrated successfully thousands of times, including making predictions to Professors and members of the academic community, much to their wonderment and astonishment. Any logical rationality they may have had goes out the window when my predictions are accurate. I have often found myself demonstrating evidence of the future in almost every reading I have ever given.

I work with past, present and future names, dates, months and years. It is all evidence. It's a way I enjoy working with Spirit because the evidence is more genuine and significant to a person. This type of evidence is important enough for clients to remember a birthday, passing or anniversary. I see current events as they happen and future events that may happen. I don't know whether this information comes from Spirit, or from my ability as a Psychic, or perhaps both. All I know is that the information is usually often very credible.

Everyone has their own views and expectations on how a Psychic or Medium should work. My fitting into someone else's ideology doesn't work for me. I need to be natural with no strings and no restrictions. I don't change anything to suit anyone. Nor do I try to animate any other Psychics or Mediums. What you see is what you get. I have my own unique 'Carole Bromley' Medium and comedian trending style when I work. And I like to swear! In a nice, funny, elegant, lady-ish sort of tongue-in-cheek-way. I sometimes wish I didn't swear so much as I do, but I think it's because of all the bullying I've been through in my life.

To be honest, I have gotten to the stage where I don't give a damn about the bullies or the sceptics. I know they don't give a ... excuse me a moment ... fuck about me, why should they? If swearing helps me to survive then so be it, no apologies needed. So please don't get offended. I know there are plenty of souls in the Spirit World who also like to have a good swear too! Besides, if I gave in to the bullies, the sceptics, and everyone else who wanted to destroy me and the good work I do, I wouldn't be able to give help that was needed to the people in need of my support. Not to mention the deceased souls who also enjoy and benefit from my conversations. I wouldn't deny anyone my help simply because someone didn't like the job I do.

Some people don't know how to be kind-hearted. Some people hate kind-hearted. So, I don't always explain what I do because I'm tired of explaining myself to people who act as a judge and form a jury.

Yet, through it all, I haven't lost my kindness, compassion, empathy, sanity, generosity or honesty with people. I'd give a person the last penny out of my purse if it helped them. But, despite it all, I'm still wearing my knickers the right way around and not inside out! I don't lose any sleep anymore. And I don't feel guilty doing what I do. In retrospect, I know there are people out there who should feel guilty in doing what they do, or perhaps more of what they don't do! God only knows I have needed strength. But Spirit, bless them, have given me strength.

Chapter 4
My Apprenticeship with Spirit

I had a lot to learn over the years about mediumship before I embraced on my life as a Medium. I learnt just how much it meant to me, too. Though I would never call myself a 'Medium,' I left that for other people to decide for themselves. It didn't seem right for me to give myself that title. Only those who knew me and those who had readings with me knew I truly was a 'Medium.' So, it made sense for me to develop mediumship, especially since I had been given this special 'gift' as a child.

As I was developing I realised I would make mistakes. I realised I wouldn't get everything right. Truth is, I never stopped developing and I never stopped making mistakes, nor did I get everything right. But, like everyone, I learnt from my mistakes through experience. We all learn from our mistakes no matter what job we do. And, we all learn from our experiences too.

I know my lessons over the years have been an experience, and that's putting it mildly. I've had the pleasure of meeting and working with good and bad Spirits. I've also experienced the same in working with good and bad people. Though, my battles and experiences as a developing Medium have been many, I've learned a great deal from ghosts, Spirits and the living. I've had to - it's been part of my job that I've trained for and who I am today. Of course, there's been the usual run-of-the-mill libellous and slanderous stuff of being a fake. Even to people who have never met me or knew me. Unfortunately, people can make you look like a fake in an instant. All it takes is for someone to press a few buttons on a computer to make a person look bloody brilliant, or in my line of business that isn't accepted by everyone, fluffy and fake! I've experienced both.

From what I know, anyone and everyone can make you look how they want you to look. People can be exceptionally clever in editing all forms of sound and vision on a multitude of platforms. TV included.

Regrettably, we cannot control how other people create, alter, or use information they have on us, receive on us, or about us. We cannot control how an innocent piece of filming is edited or used to our advantage, or to the advantage of the person creating the film. The only thing we can control is how we react. I, for one, wish anyone well (excuse me … bad cough) on anything that has been sliced and diced in any attempt to destroy me. People have tried but destroying me will never happen because people are getting much better at knowing the truth than those who alter it.

Accusations of being fake used to happen even before I had an opportunity to demonstrate the possibilities of this 'Other' life I'm a part of. I'd be accused of being a fake just by the job I do and by my profile on social media. People would draw on their own beliefs and their own conclusions.

I learnt to act a 'Fool' for the 'Fool.' You see, people would test me and laugh at me as I gave them information that was correct. I would be humiliated just because the person trying to humiliate me didn't believe in my world. I would be accused of being a fake, when in truth, it would be them a fake. Information I gave as evidence connected to them would be rejected, even though it was evidence from the soul visiting at the time. But, none of this would matter to someone who did not want to believe.

I cannot and will not force people to accept any information based on my psychic or mediumship abilities. Even though I may find out at a later date just how correct I had been. Being a Medium, I would still be fake in their mindset. I could also often be responsible for someone's five minutes of social media fame because they had something against me. Perhaps they weren't negating me as a person, but more so as a Psychic Medium. Perhaps, too, as a person of interest to those within the scientific community who cannot find proof of my Other World, or how it can be contacted.

Anyone and everyone can appear to be a seasoned critic when it comes to Mediums and the work we do. Yet the worst thing about many critics is how they suddenly know everything in a matter of minutes, or even seconds from something they've just read or seen. As with everything connected to social media, no matter who posts it, whether a cyber bully, critic or troll, their readers will believe it. But, Yay! Fortunately, many of the critics I've come across have had no idea about the subject they were criticizing – mainly due to a lack of knowledge and experience.

Now I, on the other hand, have been my own worst critic over the years. And still am. There was a time when I would think perhaps I had got it wrong. I would think perhaps there wasn't an afterlife after all. I would think perhaps it was all my imagination and perhaps I was being silly in thinking dead people spoke to me. People were closed-minded and made me feel I should be, too. I questioned everything that was thrown at me. I'm glad I did.

As an apprentice on my Spiritual journey, before I began working as a Medium, there was a part of me that I wasn't able to do. I couldn't hide the fact how deceased souls kept talking to me, how they were giving me nothing but the truth in the messages I was randomly giving to friends, and *friends of friends*.

There would be nothing in the messages that could be disputed, because the things I had referenced would be poignant and evidential. I would know about things I couldn't possibly have known. I would get things right as I heard the information being given to me, or when I saw visions that would be relevant or significant and pertaining to past, present or future events.

There was a time when I had my own website and chatroom. It was at a time when there were hardly any psychic sites up and running. There weren't too many Mediums who were well-known or famous, either. However, it was actually in one well-known TV Medium's chatroom where I began to give readings quite frequently. I was just as amazed as everyone else to know how right I was with the messages I was typing out.

Besides me, other people were also giving readings, but when my name kept being asked for I had to leave, because I was asked to. Perhaps because people were asking for me, instead of the Medium whose site it was. I was disappointed but understood. I missed giving readings. However, with the help of Hubby, I was able to soon set up a website with my own chatroom.

Using the chatroom was ideal for me to develop, as it was the start of my real apprenticeship in working with Spirit. Honestly, I was thick as shit back then-excuse my French. I was clueless as to what I was doing and why. I hadn't even actually thought about becoming a Medium. I didn't know much about Mediums or what they did, to be honest. That's how thick I was. All I knew was I was doing something that I'd always been doing. I was giving information to people, only I was engaging in conversations with them and their loved ones in Heaven. I was no longer keeping the voices to myself. I had a channel I could use to have those voices heard.

My years of training as a typist and audio typist came in handy as I sat at my computer delivering messages. Messages that felt very surreal. Instead of listening to a physical person dictating to me, I would be listening to the voice of Spirit. I would find myself in a semi-trance state of mind as the keys to my computer typed away and made words appear on the screen without my realising, and they would be accurate for the person I was delivering them to.

Don't ask me or any of the scientific 'experts' out there how it's possible to be evidential when giving internet readings that are extraordinarily accurate. Don't ask because neither of us will have an answer. Well, at least not yet, anyway. All I know is the messages I was giving in the chatroom were always significant and important to the person receiving the information. Furthermore, it proved loved ones still watch over us no matter where we are - even in a chatroom on a computer. And of course, frequent visitations don't stop the conversations just because I visit the loo. For some weird reason, I can have quite a few loo chats with disembodied voices and spirits. I do laugh, but, honestly, no shame!

Irrespective of my talking to dead people and working with them, it wasn't something I even wanted. I tried to ignore the disembodied voices and their presence as much as I could, for as long as I could. But I couldn't. I even had a minister from the Spiritualist church come to close me down, to stop Spirit contacting me - three times no less. As you can see, that didn't go very well. Spirit, bless 'em, were adamant enough to keep head-hunting me to work for them. As the saying goes, 'If you can't beat 'em, join 'em'. And I did exactly that. I had to.

I also had to do this for my unborn son, Simon. I lost Simon (the name I gave him) following a procedure for IVF (In-Vitro Fertilisation). I had IVF because it was our last hope. Unfortunately, it wasn't meant to be, and we lost our baby. Knowing I'd never have kids left me with an empty feeling. I would often suffer from bouts of sadness at not living my life as a physical Mother or a Grandmother.

Suffering with cysts on my fallopian tubes and ovaries is something I have endured over many years. I've had a fair few operations to drain the bastards, too. I remember having a cyst on my leg as a kid. I remember, too, how bloody painful it was. Now, my ovaries are stuck to my bowel, so that's another shitty problem to be sorted when the time comes. I still have lumps and bumps in my left leg. And if I didn't know any better, I'd laugh and think aliens took me and experimented on me at some time in my life. But, if they did, they could have asked permission first. Please, I'm not serious with this alien stuff. It's just good to make light of something so difficult.

However, with Simon, I am his earthly Spiritual Mother. And, I remember quite clearly the day when he crawled up on my lap. I was feeling rock bottom and fed up with my life and some of the people in it. We can get like that, can't we? Even though I loved my day job, I wasn't even happy there. I was at a point in my life where all I knew is how I wanted nothing more to do with Spirit, dead people, and helping people - until a visit from Simon told me different.

During Simon's visitation, I could feel his energy as he put his tiny arms around my neck and hugged me. He whispered in my ear, "Please don't give up Mummy, we need you." I burst out crying. How could I not help? I knew I couldn't have a physical family, but I knew we had a lovely son growing up in Heaven. I also knew my sister would be looking after our son.

Whilst I may not have been able to physically hold Simon in my arms, I knew I could love him in another way. I could love him between our worlds through sending my thoughts to him. I could love him because I knew there was a Heaven and people didn't just die. The evidence I had been given from deceased souls in the Spirit World contradicted this theory. There is more to life than the life we know. We will all be part of this 'Other' life when we get to Heaven. We will all see how it does exist and how we are a part of it. Forget about school reunions, these reunions are far better.

Anyway, Simon, as a Spirit soul and energy himself, knew how much it meant for deceased souls to reunite with family and friends, he was a Spirit himself. He had reunited with me, his Mother. Simon knew this was what I was meant to do, work with Spirit. I know that, too. No Mum lets their kids down - and I wasn't going to let my Simon down. No way was I giving up. I was going to be an Ambassador and a voice for each and every Spirit soul I would connect and have a conversation with. I was going to bring two worlds together, regardless of the battles I had endured with disbelievers.

Despite all my horrible health issues, I muddled through, as you do. The battles from other people were many, and my day job was very demanding. I managed both my work and my paranormal hobby for as long as could.

However, I knew the day would come when I would have to decide between working at the office for someone else or working for Spirit.

I would contemplate my future quite often, until one day when the answer was sent to me directly from Spirit itself. I sometimes got these strange, unexplained feelings when I knew something was going to happen to me. I would get, as I still do, a strange anxious feeling whenever I knew Spirit was going to tell me something important that was important to me. I knew because the palm of my hand would tingle. This anxious energy I felt would usually be from Spirit themselves or from one of my Spirit Guides. All I knew was that whenever I got this type of feeling I would really have to pay special attention. I did exactly that when I made the decision to give up my day job at the University and work only for Spirit. It was a huge risk, but I'm glad I listened.

My apprenticeship with Spirit over the past two decades has included everything from developing Mediumship to Transfiguration. My development has also included Trance Mediumship, although the latter method is not a preference I use too often. This is because I enjoy Psychic Mediumship the most. As an apprentice and developing Medium, though, I was always open to using many ways of communicating with Spirit.

Since I was also a Paranormal Investigator, I would often investigate locations with a team of paranormal investigators. I would also often hold a séance and use 'Spirit of the Glass.' Spirit of the Glass is a method of communication using letters of the alphabet scattered around a table. A glass would be placed in the middle where our finger tips would gently rest and allow Spirit to move the glass. It would move across the table spelling out words to questions asked, or at times, spell out their own message. Please do NOT try this method if you have no experience in opening or closing a séance. There can be serious consequences if a Spirit chooses to stay.

As a Paranormal Investigator, I found out how not all venues are haunted. Some venues do really well for ghost hunting, even though they have no ghost (entities that become attached to a place or location). One venue I did investigate that was definitely haunted was at Syon Park House. I was privileged and honoured to investigate Syon House, Isleworth, owned by the Duke and Duchess of Northumberland. It was once the residence of Lady Jane Grey (1537-1554). Sadly, Lady Jane Grey was Queen of England for only nine days before her execution at the Tower of London.

Staff at the house had witnessed for themselves paranormal activity that could not be explained. I investigated Syon House on a few occasions. This was also the secret location that I mention in chapter eighteen, 'Haunted Footsteps' in my first book. Except now, it's not a secret anymore. Since I was invited three years running to host Ghost Tours in the house, usually around Halloween, I was able to speak and disclose my findings in the house as a Paranormal Investigator.

Syon House, I can honestly say is not a place where I would enjoy spending a night. I'd never get any sleep for a start. There is far too much spiritual activity that makes staying awake interesting. Examples of some of this activity ranged from the fire alarm going off to disembodied voices being heard, a chair being moved on its own in the dining room, footsteps in the corridors, and someone kicking the sofa from behind in one of the rooms. But, before all you ghost investigators pick up the phone and start enquiring about your own investigation at this place, DON'T. Syon House does not permit paranormal investigators. I was fortunate enough to make the call at the right time. No further investigations needed. Personally, I would do it again myself if they gave permission, but they won't. Please, understand, it's not just a house, it's a well-preserved home too.

Putting aside everything I was experimenting with whilst working with Spirit, I knew how this apprenticeship I had entered into for the purpose of developing Mediumship was going to be a long haul. I didn't mind, though

- I would be ready when I was ready. It really was going to be a huge milestone for me in working with *dead* people. I had to learn to trust in myself, in Spirit and the people I would be having conversations with and giving messages to.

My trust from Spirit had to be one hundred percent - because they were the one's I was relying on to get the information right. They were the ones who trusted me to deliver their memories as accurate as possible and share their love. It was my duty to provide evidence that would be helpful and healing not just to them, but to those they wanted to connect to as well.

In my early days of development, I learned how the work of a Medium and what I was doing wasn't going to be everyone's cup of tea. I learned how some people wouldn't be my cup of tea, either. I got that. Oddly enough, I've had a few messages given to me from people asking, 'What planet are you on?' or telling me, 'It's rubbish what you do' more times than I can remember. I've also been obliged to give them a message back. But, my own version, of course, not Spirit's!

Even though it was soul destroying, I got used to being laughed at. Mostly because I accepted how people didn't understand me, my work, and what I do. I grew to learn how people's reactions in my talking to dead people were all part of the job. I learned how it would be based on my own understanding of how much people knew about an afterlife, and how much they would, or wouldn't accept there's no such thing as being 'dead'.

It was crazy how people would laugh at me before they got to know me. I would tell myself it was okay, when it wasn't. I wasn't OKAY! I would tell myself they didn't know what I know because they hadn't experienced the same as I had. I remember how people made me look and feel stupid, intentionally. Those were the most difficult days, weeks, months and years of my life. I'm so blessed to not give a (close your eyes rude word coming up!) fuck anymore.

Honestly, there would be many more times when I wanted to walk away from using my psychic ability and talking to dead people. I wanted to walk away from reuniting families in both worlds. I would think there was no point in doing this work if people kept having a go at me when I tried so hard to help people and their deceased souls heal. But I couldn't, nor wouldn't, give up this incredible journey I was chosen to do and made to feel a part of. I wouldn't give up because each time I would remember what Simon had told me.

I took comfort in telling myself these people who didn't believe me didn't know any different. They didn't know what was real about an afterlife and what wasn't - they hadn't worn my shoes. I stuck it out with all the laughs the same way I stuck it out with the cyber bullying and harassment. I stuck with knowing how my world of Spirit and talking to dead people was not something everyone could accept or even experience.

Developing Mediumship was something I had to learn by myself and with discarnate souls. It was a role we had to learn together. It wasn't something I could ask other people to help me with. You can only have one person driving a car, and this was my car. I learned to change gears according to the speed I was developing. I revved up the motor when the motor needed revving. There were no short cuts on this road. I certainly drove through the 'School of Hard Knocks.' which I totally appreciated because it shaped me into the professional Medium and person I am today.

I have had to learn to overcome the many battles of scepticism and criticism. I fought battles with 'Ghosts, Spirits and The Living.' It's not easy to explain to people how possible it is to work with someone who is dead. All I know is that believing in an afterlife is to be open to the possible, instead of the impossible. There may, too, come a day when someone from Heaven comes knocking at your door, if they haven't already! And, like me, it will be up to you if you choose to open that door or close it.

The Spirit World is a place that has existed since man has existed, and where souls have continued to migrate. It is a dimension that cannot be destroyed, blown up, sunk, poisoned, melted or blasted out of the universe. Neither can any soul of a Spirit be destroyed, as it is an intelligent energy and eternal life force.

Since there is so much a Spirit soul can do, we should not underestimate its intelligence, or its power. Instead, we should be embracing its intelligence and learning something different and deeper about who they are. We should be learning something about who we really are.

Spirit souls are constantly evolving. They are of a far more superior intelligent form of life than any other living species. There is so much they have learnt in ways to connect and communicate with us that the Spirit World itself is evolving with us. We are all evolving together. Mediums and Mediumship is evolving. As a Medium, I am proud to evolve with deceased souls and loved ones who are all connected to the GOD source, the SPIRIT WORLD and ONE consciousness.

I believe the Spirit World has its own platform that we can all connect to and be a part of. I know this dimension is the same special place I have evolved in over decades. If it weren't so funny, I'd say it's probably about the only place I have ever evolved, to be honest.

Chapter 5
All Work and No Play

My career and working roles over the years have been … interesting. Chequered and varied but interesting none the less. I really do mash up a good read as far as what I've done, but, like me, I'm sure you'll be amazed at just exactly what I have done. One thing for certain was that I never envisioned myself working as a Psychic Medium. It was never a thought let alone an ambition. Yet, somehow it has ended up on my Curriculum Vitae.

I've had many roles to endure since my Saturday jobs at Tesco and Woolworths, from the age of fourteen to sixteen. My efforts since leaving school in keeping a regular job truly had been quite dismal. I had worked for quite a few companies and failed in keeping a job. I've also never had a career break throughout my working life. To be honest, there has been some jobs where I felt I was never meant to be there. Wherever 'there' was. Perhaps because people thought I had a strange look about me or didn't understand me – that would make sense. I just didn't feel as though I fitted in. I was different, people may have noticed this and therefore treated me differently. Different to the point of being an outsider. I often felt I was the dumping ground for other people's shitty jobs – jobs too mundane or too boring.

In retrospect, I can honestly say in almost every job I have ever had there was always someone who stopped me from getting a well-deserved promotion. I may have also lost or given up a job because I was really crap at what I was supposed to do, in which case, I certainly didn't need or deserve to be there. People can be funny … in a horrible way. It took a long time for me to realise how it was *their* problem not mine.

Nonetheless, besides being a Medium, the only other job I was truly passionate about was my time as a Disc Jockey. I'd always been interested in records and pop music from an early age. I even bought my first record when I was only eleven years old. I didn't stop there either as I had my own disco unit and thousands of records by the time I reached my twenties.

My budding career as a disc jockey started when I was sixteen. I was a volunteer at Hospital Radio Hillingdon. The hospital was at the top of my road, so it was only a short distance. I could walk there quite easily. Each week, I would count the days until I was there again. I would run out of the school gates every Wednesday afternoon, heading home to have a quick snack before getting ready to go to the studio.

It wasn't long before I was hosting and producing my own radio request show. I had a lot of strange requests in records from patients. And, I could guarantee every week without fail I would get a request for Jim Reeves' 'Distant Drums', Led Zeppelin's 'Stairway to Heaven' or Rod Stewart's 'The First Cut is the Deepest'. I'll leave you to ponder over those song choices!

Looking back, I really was lucky I got a break into the music business. It led to bigger opportunities for me. I progressed from hospital radio to working as a club DJ in the early 1980s. My cousins, Alton and Tony worked for an agent in Denmark. Their agent was looking to recruit female jocks. Something I could help with. Through my cousins the agent offered me a job. I literally had one week to get a passport, pack my bags and organise my record collection. I had loads of records filling three suitcases, with just a small vanity case for a few of my clothes. If it weren't for the records I would have been travelling light. But, as long as I had my records, I didn't really care what I was wearing.

I was twenty-one and going to live and work in an unfamiliar country.

It was exciting. I was excited. Mum wasn't pleased, though, it broke her heart. It was a hard decision for me to make, but I couldn't turn down a job I was passionate about.

I couldn't speak the Danish lingo, but then I didn't need to. Even though the language was hard to learn, I got to know how to order a beer. I also became an expert at swearing in Danish, as well as in English. Anyway, nearly everyone I spoke to wanted to practice their English on me, so learning Danish was hard. Besides that, I was sleeping all day so never really got an opportunity meeting too many people. I never got an opportunity where I could pick up and learn the language as much as I'd like to have done. I got by. I just needed to spin the records and do the job I loved. Mum would understand.

During my time in Denmark I had acquired thirteen suitcases – Yes, you read that right! Thirteen bloody heavy suitcases filled with a few more clothes, records and a collection of souvenirs. I didn't drive, even though I had to change clubs monthly. No DJ worked the same club for more than a month, two at the most. Don't even ask how I managed with all the suitcases, but I managed.

Nationally and internationally, I was a professional working female Disc Jockey which was rare in the 1980s. I also remember how I worked mostly in a drunken stupor. Drinks were free and flowed. I flowed - Yay! I was young and lived life to the full. Times have changed. I may be older and wiser, but I still have plenty of 'Spirit' in me, yet. Pardon the pun and point me to the nearest pub!

Prior to carrying out contracts working in Denmark, I had also worked for Juliana's in Kensington, a well-known International entertainment agency employing top professional disc jockeys. I was proud to be one of their jocks for a year as a resident DJ at Runnymede Hotel, Egham, near Windsor. It was after my contract at Runnymede came to an end that I sailed off to Denmark.

I actually saw more of Denmark than I did of England. Even though the social scene was the highlight of my career, getting into drunken stupors and working every night just wasn't fun anymore. After two and half years, I left to return back home to England.

Getting a normal job after DJ'ing for so long was really hard. No one wanted to employ a disc jockey. Unless, the job itself required one. I didn't want to be a DJ, I wanted to work in an office, like all my other friends. I just didn't have enough experience or skills. Getting back into a routine of sleeping at night and staying awake during the day was also hard. The night shifts as a DJ mucked up my body system and sleep pattern. I also found it difficult to keep any job I was lucky to land, so mostly temped where I could.

I was fortunate I could choose my own hours while temping, especially when my Dad got ill. I would visit Dad in hospital and sit with him daily. He had been diagnosed with lung cancer and had just a few weeks to live. I was shocked. We were all shocked because we had no idea he was so ill. Dad, himself, didn't realise just how ill he was, let alone have cancer and was dying. I remember how his wife, Meg, had rushed to the hospital and how she didn't know the seriousness of his condition. It was only when I pulled her away from Dad's bedside and asked her if she had spoken to his Doctors that I realised she hadn't. No one had told her she was going to lose her husband. I told her. It was a moment of disbelief.

Dad was scared, I was scared for him. I was scared for me, too, because I was losing my Dad. Thankfully, the temporary work I had at the time was handy. I chose not to work, but instead, be with Dad as much as I could. This gave both of us comfort knowing we could be with each other during his last days. Something I couldn't possibly have done had I been permanently employed by a company. Family is more important than any job. Companies can replace you, but you can't replace your family. I treasured the time I could spend with my Dad.

I've had a variety of jobs and roles over the years - and working as a waitress and washer-upper in a very greasy café was just one of them. I've operated heavy industrial machinery on a factory floor that made bellows for radiators. I exchanged my greasy overalls for a shirt and skirt when I was promoted to an office clerk within the same company. Not to mention working as a check-out-chic at Tesco's.

However, I don't believe in coincidences, but, I even managed to get a job inspecting records at Island Records before going on to work as a full-time professional DJ. I even managed a smile at Steven Spielberg as we crossed on the stairs when I was temping as a secretary at Technicolor. There were many nights, too, when I'd go home stinking of cigarette smoke and beer from pulling pints and mixing Spirits as a barmaid. I'm still good at mixing Spirits, just not the ones in bottles!

I was also employed by Apple Computer UK, as the Sale's Director's secretary. Whilst I was there, I had begun to learn the Tarot cards. The Managing Director noticed my cards spread across my desk one day as he walked past. Just as well it was my lunch hour. Anyway, he told me to go to his office and bring the cards with me. I hated how he had noticed. I thought he was going to tell me of! thankfully, he didn't. With a smile on his face he said "Carole, I want you to read my cards." I was nervous as I told him "I'm only learning, I need to use the book." He laughed, I laughed. I gave him a reading anyway.

After almost two years, I was made redundant from Apple with quite a few others. I ducked and dived doing a bit here and a bit there wherever I could for work. Then I landed a job at Sony Colnbrook. At 11:00am every morning, I would hear a Concorde take off from Heathrow Airport. I would be standing outside smoking a cigarette (something I have since given up) as the earth shook beneath me, literally. My role was as an Administrator, until the company was taken over and relocated to a different area. It was a pity I had to leave, but I couldn't get transport or relocate to the new location. Another job bit the dust.

I was back on the books with an agency temping again. I didn't have to wait long before they offered me a post as a temp working for a local company. Yay! The contract offered was at Brunel University in Uxbridge, on the outskirts of London. No interview required. Double Yay!

To be honest, I never got a job through being interviewed, anyway. I was hopeless at interviews and conversations that meant talking about me. Many jobs I ever had were mostly from temp-to-perm, kind of try before you buy. I am more of a hands-on person than a paper trail person. I hated filling out forms indicating what I could and couldn't do. I've never been good with words, so a 'kiss and tell all' application form never led to any employment.

Anyway, I had a job at the Uni. I was contracted in the role for three weeks within the Human Resources department. This turned into a few months. Before I knew it, a few years had rolled-by with more contracts for numerous jobs in various departments. I surprised myself. I know those up there in the Spirit World had helped me get into the University for a reason. I know they kept me employed there, too. It was the biggest and most challenging experience of my working life. I had many reasons to be there and I loved being there.

Although I liked what I was doing, it didn't stop me feeling like a fraud. I had no degree nor certificates to shove around a desk. Perhaps a few too I would have shoved up someone's arse! I had nothing that would suggest I was qualified, or good enough for the roles I was employed to do. I seemed to manage, and for fifteen years I managed. Yet, I was never without work whilst working at the University, and I never had a break between any contract. Spiritual and Divine intervention were certainly at work. God bless them because they certainly blessed me.

I had some interesting roles at the University which I was able to settle into. Some contracts were longer than others, but at least I was employed. Most of those contracts were Personal Assistant related. I would do this type of work by day - then change hats into a developing Medium by night. I had been a developing Medium for a good five years before my fifteen-year life sentence ended at the University.

It was whilst I was working at Brunel that I started to predominantly lead and enjoy more of a double-life. I wasn't exactly masquerading as Mrs. Bond, nor did I work for MI5, and I certainly wasn't one of Charlie's Angels, either. I can't speak for 'Charlie', but I did put a lot of effort into being an Angel ... I think! Put it this way, I had a double-life where I was a rose amongst many thorns.

It was also at the University where I had the idea to write my first non-fiction book, 'The Living Spirit, One Woman's Battle Amongst Ghosts, Spirits & The Living,' (2009). Professor Ray J Paul (Dean of Systems Engineering) whom I worked for as a Personal Assistant helped me where he could. The Professor also published his own book, 'Living with Parkinson's, Shake, Rattle & Roll' (2009). We launched our books at the same time. Additionally, Professor Fay Weldon, CBE who was also one of my invited speakers at the book launch, also gave me some valuable advice regarding writing a book. I was lucky she gave me time. I was able to schedule a few meetings to discuss the format of my book with her. I really appreciated both the Professor's help and advice.

Writing my book had taken me six years, mostly because I was dyslexic, which I hid quite well. I would get words the wrong way around or miss words out. It was exasperating. I also had no idea how authors wrote, so putting a paragraph together was frustrating. Stringing a sentence together was nauseating. But, to be honest, I just wrote and threw all the writing and publishing rules out the window. So, God bless you if you are still reading my story. Professional hired help cost money. I couldn't afford the fees. That in itself is a huge drawback for those who want to be an Author. There's a lot of talent out there, like me, with lack of funds and unable to get a publisher.

I learned to balance my life and my two working roles. By day I worked at the University; by night, training as a Medium. When my contract ended working for Professor Paul I moved across to the Graduate School. It was here I worked as a PA to the Dean. This role stayed the same for me when the Pro-Vice Chancellor of the Graduate School took over and I remained as his PA for a while.

I knew whilst I was working at the University that if I worked hard in developing Mediumship, then I could one day work for the Spirit World full time. It was a huge commitment for me to dedicate time and effort into both jobs, but I did. My passion was intense – my passion was no fad, or five-minute wonder I was going through. It was something happening to me that took place over more than twenty years. Even longer if you count back to when I was six years old with the crazy clown and the disembodied voices talking to me.

At the time of leaving the University in 2014, I had spent the last five years as Project Manager salaried by the European Commission. It was an interesting role I grew out of, or it grew out of me. I had no regrets about leaving, and in fact, I was quite excited because I was leaving to work as a full-time, self-employed, professional Psychic Medium. I can't tell you how much I looked forward to working my last day at the University.

People and promises have flown past me over the years but have never stopped to deliver. You know, those who want to help but do nothing. There was always someone, somewhere who wanted to help me by introducing me to the right people - or doing things that would benefit my work and get my name out there. When in reality, they could do nothing. To be honest, I have had more faith in Santa Claus, at least he delivers. My hopes and expectations have often been dampened through false promises by fake people. I have learnt not to expect anything from anyone. I'm proud of my own accomplishments, and I'm doing well.

My life as a Psychic Medium couldn't be any better. People come to me on their own accord. Those who do come to me are the ones I care about. People's loved ones in Heaven are the ones I care about. They are the reason I do this work. Spirit and I give people a lot of good memories to cherish. We give people hope when they could see none. We change people's lives because change is needed. We remove the clouds and replace them with the sun. This is my job, I am proud of my job and my life. I'm a Psychic and a Medium, I am employed by Spirit. I'm proud to add that to my Curriculum Vitae.

Chapter 6
Employed with Spirit

My relationship with the Spirit World is one of loyalty and confidentiality. It is one based on trust. It can be funny, demanding, heart-breaking, emotional, hilarious, serious stuff, take-over-your-life, and sometimes a very scary type of relationship. Representing both worlds comes with a huge amount of responsibility. Did I say it is also hard-working, too? It is. But I wouldn't have it any other way.

As you can imagine, it's not an easy thing to admit to, in working for an employer that is out of this world. I'd get frowned upon. And naturally, I'd frown back. People looked at me, I looked at them. Sometimes, I could tell they were embarrassed. Not sure if they were embarrassed they'd asked what I did for a living, or for me doing a job that wasn't the 'norm.'

If I heard it once, I heard it a thousand times on how I should get a 'proper' job. Especially more so in my early years when I was engaging as an apprentice in developing Mediumship. I didn't see what the problem was, I had a proper job, but still people wanted me to stop dabbling with death. I wouldn't stop. I was on a mission. I kept on going despite the hurtful comments. It was my world, not theirs. They didn't understand. It was a hurdle I needed to get my leg over, throw my feet in front of me, literally, before I could stand up, straighten my skirt, and follow my own yellow brick road.

I would be so embarrassed talking about GOD or The Spirit World because of the stigma of religion associated with it. I would shun anything that had religion written anywhere near it. I learned how the Spirit World is a place we ALL go to, so it's not religious. My reference to a *GOD* source is something that is a Universal omnipresent force that people can relate to, for any or many reasons. I'm not religious, I'm just happy as I am; a totally free independent Spirit 'Employed with Spirit.'

I have a good understanding about my lifelong commitment and employment with the Spirit World. For a start, it really is eternal. Needless to say, it's also one of those roles whereby I will never ever be made redundant or sacked. Nor will I ever be bullied or taken for granted. Too many people are consumed in a negative work environment for my liking. An environment that is bad for their health. It's shocking. I don't aim to join any of them, or work for anyone who has no respect for the people who work exceptionally hard, try to do a job and earn a decent living at the same time. Every work environment should be a lovely, happy and healthy place to be and to want to be.

In my experience of over two decades in working for the Spirt World, I can tell you, it's not always easy. There's more to their world than them popping up all over the place. There's more to this work than them, Spirit, visiting to have conversations with their loved ones, believe it or not. There are parts of my job that people don't get to see or understand. If only they could. When people see me as a Medium, they see me giving messages. That's all they see. There is so much more than communicating with deceased souls and giving messages. There is much more responsibility that comes with my work as a Psychic Medium to both the 'living' and the 'dead.' Yet, regrettably, the work that I do can easily be dismissed, judged and misjudged, often by those who know nothing of this other world I am a part of, or of the pain that lives on with those who have loved and lost.

I can get into a few conversations with those who think they know everything about discarnate souls and the Spirit World. Yet, really know dip shit! Honestly! I have nothing to argue about when someone is trying to converse with me who hasn't experienced something of what I do. There is no point in having a debate or argument when it's going to be one-sided. The result is always going to be the same, a no-win situation.

I'm the one who sees and hears evidence of deceased souls from the Spirit World every single day of the year. But for those who haven't experienced this world and disrespect it, all I can say is it's a bit like you trying to explain to me how you like, or dislike Paris as a country - but not a clue what it's like not having been there. I am reasonable, but I have a strong attention deficit when it comes to people who only *think* they know about Paris without experiencing the culture. I have little respect for those who claim to know everything about my job and my extraordinary world, without having experienced it first-hand.

In my world I demonstrate survival of the consciousness in an afterlife. I have never at any time in my life thought for one minute once you're *dead* your *dead* – end of. No! What a horrible thought, not to mention a horrible empty feeling. I know that when I get to Heaven I can come back and visit my family and friends. I know how there are many ways I can get a message to someone I love. And if the only way I could get a message or evidence of my existence in the afterlife was through a Medium, then so be it. I would want to make myself known. I'd have fun tapping on a few doors to get someone's attention in the process. So, let's not knock it. Instead, embrace the work and effort that goes on in both worlds, not just by Mediums, but by those who BELIEVE, too.

Now I've got this far, and as you know, I never had a really good track record in keeping myself employed, my resume indicates that. But, after my time was over working at Brunel, I literally swore I would never work for any other employer. I only wanted to work for the Spirit World. After all, I'd spent my life growing up amongst those who visited me from that world. I wanted more than ever to work with dead people, Spirit souls, their family and friends when and where I could. The Spirit World and the Heavenly realms were the right 'Company' for me to work for. It was my calling. They were my calling.

I have spent over twenty years in training as a Medium, (I've been psychic since birth) that's longer than a graduate would spend at University working towards a degree. So, I can hardly be a fake. I am a graduate in my own right. I have earned my own degree in recognition for the work I do with discarnate souls and the Spirit World. I am working for the right employer, with the right attitude. I am working for an employer who wants the best for me ... Carole Bromley. I am working for an employer who wants the best for everyone, no matter which world we live in.

Abundant thanks and blessings to every one of you out there who have helped me on my journey, so far. Because of you, your support has also helped Spirit and your deceased loved ones, too. You have made their existence with their memories and love matter. You have helped to open up the Spirit World not only to your heart, but to a wider audience. You have helped yourself and your deceased loved ones to heal. We are grateful to you. Blessings to you. Our job is love and of love. To love, give love and be loved. We all deserve love. Thank you for sharing yours.

My induction period for being 'Employed with Spirit' is now over and I have graduated with a few feathers, an abundance of knowledge and a wealth of experience. I still have more degrees and feathers to earn because the learning never stops. The Spirit World has been looking after me because I look after those who are in it. I have been trusted to do their work. What an honour and a blessing to work for a large place in our space in the Spirit World. Thank You.

Unless you've seen me 'LIVE' and alive with your own eyes, you haven't really seen me. You don't really know me. You know nothing of what I do, or who I am. This thing I have, it is what it is. My journey ... is one complete with warts. I have nothing to hide. I am learning every day just like everyone else. I take responsibility for any past, present and future actions. I am an 'Open Book' literally. I am a Psychic Medium, Reiki Teacher, Past Life Regressionist, Spiritual Teacher, Oracle Card Reader and Author. I am Carole Bromley, a person, and I'm blessed in ALL that I do with this work. I am proud of what I do and the healing I bring.

Chapter 7
Psychic Medium

I chose to work as a Medium because I couldn't seem to get rid of or ignore all the Spirit souls who were asking for my help. The whispering of disembodied voices never stopped. I have always felt compelled to help the souls behind the voices as part of my duty. I am their Ambassador, I am their voice. I reunite departed souls with their loved ones. This is the work I do that I want to share with you.

Because my work is mostly evidence based, I have to do the best I can, specifically when it comes to getting accurate information from departed souls. Evidential information I have learned to use as a Psychic Medium include (but is not limited to) names, dates of birthdays, anniversaries, passing's, house numbers, people's ages, events, relationships, deaths, physical conditions, symptoms, signs and symbols, the future, and more. I am also a Physical Medium, too, which I cover in Physical Mediumship (chapter Eight).

As a Medium, I have no idea what is going to happen when I'm working. I have no idea who I will be talking to, either. It's probably going to be just as much a surprise to me as it is for the client and person sitting in front of me, or persons I am working with. This is because many of the mechanics of mediumship can work in a variety of ways, as this chapter will explain.

It goes without saying how deceased relatives and friends alike never disappoint to connect to those who once mattered. They never disappoint to visit those who come to communicate at the time of the reading. Furthermore, any link being made can often expand and connect to people other than the client sitting in front of me. Literally, anything's possible when I'm working with Spirit. For instance, I recall one link I was connected to when I read for Kelly, a client of mine. She sat through the whole reading accepting everything I was giving to her. She was smiling and nodding as she made lots of notes. I was pleased for her. She went away perfectly happy when she shouldn't have been, technically.

It was a few weeks later I found out how Kelly didn't really connect to much of what was said during her reading. It was only because of Lisa, a client of mine who recommended Kelly that I got to hear about her strange experience. What I heard initially stunned me. I was perplexed. I didn't understand why someone would sit through a reading connecting to all the information and not say anything. I had one of those head-scratching moments where the reading I had given I thought had been good. I couldn't understand how it hadn't made sense. I had no idea why she paid me either. If it was me, I wouldn't have paid anyone for a reading that didn't make sense.

Fortunately, my reputation remained intact as Lisa told me how Kelly had showed her husband the notes she had made. He was shocked. It turned out the information was all related to him and his side of the family. The memories her husband's deceased loved ones gave during the reading wouldn't have been understood by Kelly, as she hadn't met her husband during those memory moments. Her husband, by the way, was a total sceptic until he met me - indirectly - through the reading with his wife. Honestly, you couldn't make this stuff up.

It's good to know how it's not only your living physical family and friends who can be nosey and want to see and hear *everything*. You also need to be aware how you've got family and friends in the Spirit World who are just as nosey and want to know almost ... everything! There's no holding them back when they want to see and listen in on your conversations, or anybody else's for that matter. And the good thing is, you just wouldn't have a clue who was listening in on you or watching you. So, it's worth noting, if you've talked about it or thought about it - someone you know over there in the Spirit World will bring it up in conversation. What's more, it's evidence how they were with you at that very moment. It's something that is always good to know, because quite often we want them to know what's going on. All we do is just save ourselves a stamp on the envelope to let them know.

Funnily enough, there have been many times where I've had to stop a conversation with Spirit because a client has asked, "Did they really see me do that?" or "Did they really know I said that?" All I know is that if I'm saying it, your deceased loved one has seen and heard it. What's more, it's evidence they were with you at that moment.

I've often seen my client's eyes light up, too, when I tell them of a song being played on the radio whilst driving on the way over to see me. But, don't worry, it's not something I can do all the time. You will only get to hear of something when I hear it. I can also tell you how secrets never die with anyone. Quite often what somebody did or said can be resurrected from the grave. The evidence spills out in the message during any conversation from a visiting loved one.

Being in the world of Spirit doesn't change anyone's personality, or the type of person they were, and still are. My clients will often tell me, "That's exactly how my mum would say it." Even down to the gestures of my hands, face, eye motions and body movement – all mimic the soul communicating memories. I have also had the pleasure of working with some very cheeky and naughty minded Spirits. A sense of humour is something that is far from lost in the afterlife. Sometimes, I see how there's a lot more sense of humour with the souls in the afterlife than we have here on the earth plane.

This is all to say, from the messages I get from deceased souls, I know how they remember everything and everybody. They are good. I mean really good. They never forget a birthday, anniversary or passing. I proved this point during a message at one of my shows. It was when I was working with a Spirit lady in giving a message to her daughter in law. A specific date had popped up. We all thought the message was going really well until I made a reference to April 9th as being important. The lady looked at me puzzled as she said, "No, sorry, I can't take that." Hmmm, I knew what I heard, and I knew she could take it. So, I asked her again and repeated the date. It still wasn't accepted. All I could do was ask her to keep it in her 'Halo!' I gestured drawing a halo above her head with my hand.

I never change dates and I don't allow dates to be changed by the person receiving them. Whether the date makes sense to them or not, I want to connect to my date because it's the date given from Spirit. As it happened, before I had finished the message, the lady's face lit up as she burst out laughing. Filled with both embarrassment and excitement she shouted, "I remembered! April 9th is my husband's birthday!" Yay! The penny dropped. Phew! We do work hard! The laughter and round of applause from the audience was extremely welcomed. It wouldn't have done for her to miss her own husband's birthday. Worse still, it wouldn't have done to upset her Mother-in-Law either. Dead or alive. People have trouble remembering even the simplest of dates when put on the spot. But, hey - was this date hot or what?! Thank God for Mother-in-Laws.

Working as a Medium, I have learned to understand how everything a client needs to know will be in the message and the conversation we will have. I have also learned how frustrating it can be for a client who wants to know something specific which may not come up during their reading. So, here's the thing; I can only say what I'm given. I can't make stuff up, so if it's not there, it's not there. Nothing I can do. Unfortunately, I don't have the answers to everything, I only wished I did. At least I would know how it might perhaps help. I always want to help, of course I do.

People's expectations in how much they want to hear during a reading can be unhealthy. I've known clients to 'throw toys out of the pram' when Mother or Grandmother and others don't step forward. Regrettably, there are times when I truly can't help. But thankfully, most of my clients are appreciative in accepting the love of the ones who do step forward for them.

Unfortunately, too, it's not my choice who visits and who doesn't - that choice belongs to your loved ones. When a client has a mindset to accept only one person who doesn't make it, everything else in the reading goes out the window. All the information that was given becomes uninteresting, redundant, yet somehow poignant. All I know is, whatever a client needs to hear will be heard. The information comes from Spirit, not me. I'm just the Messenger.

I have a great deal of empathy for all the deceased souls I work with. And I always get to know each soul through the time we connect with one another. And, because we have such a short time together, I need information that gives my client the evidence needed. I also need to know my clients will feel different after a reading I need to know the information I gave could only have come from the person they knew to be giving it. Because of this, they know their loved one truly does continue to watch over and love them.

However, I can't do a reading without preparation with every client I see. So, before each client arrives and a reading takes place, I always ask for my Spirit guide, Hannah, to step forward. Hannah is always in the room with me whenever and wherever I work. I will ask Hannah to help those in the Spirit World step forward to connect to those coming to see me. I will offer a prayer of protection against negative energies and negative Spirits. I will also ask for evidence of the past as a memory link, a link to the present, and an insight into future influences and energies to come that are relevant, helpful and healing to each and every one of my clients and their visitors.

It goes without saying, not all deceased souls can show themselves. It mostly depends on how much energy the soul has. There are times when I only get to see a face, foot, an arm, leg, the top or bottom part of the body. I may only get to see the front or back of a deceased soul. However, anything I can use in a description I will. Additionally, any form of description can be quite significant when describing a physical disability or in describing how the soul passed, including being found on the floor, in a chair, hung by the neck, stabbed in the chest etc. It's not all nice, of course it's not. Sometimes the deceased soul may not want to show themselves visually but prefer to work with voice communication only. And not all souls want to relive the memory on how they passed. Understandable.

Further evidence I get through conversations in a reading with Spirit can come from using a 'virtual' screen. This is where I visualise a TV screen in situ between myself and my client. This screen allows Spirit to use their energy to manifest and project images, symbols and words that I can use to translate into a message. So, together with the use of the screen I can use clairaudience (clear hearing), or clairvoyance (clear seeing). They both work really well together.

When I am ready to work and ready to receive Spirit, I will open my imaginary door I call my spirit door. The door is always to the right of me because this is where spirit visitations happen. This is when I start to feel their energy and hear their voice. By the way, the voices I hear are either outside my head, in my thoughts, or sometimes both.

It goes without saying, I need Spirit to trust me as much as I trust them. We are both strangers meeting for the first time. A bit like a blind date, if you like. So, it's always important for both of us to form a beautiful bond whilst we get to know and work with one another. Then I need *them* to speak to me by giving me information to start the conversation. Sometimes, Spirit, when they visit, will announce who they are by giving an indication of their relationship to my client. Alternatively, they may give a month or date that is significant. However, if this doesn't happen then it's up to me to start the conversation. No conversation ever got anywhere without someone leading it. I need to lead if it's something I need to do. Additionally, the speed of information during the reading is also important. There's nothing worse than sitting and waiting for a visitor from the Spirit World to talk. Boring! It's exactly the same situation when you're with someone and they don't talk, too. Boring! I don't do that. I like to engage with my spirit visitors. I talk to anyone, so am always keen to start a conversation with both the living and the dead.

Spirit also need to like me as much as I like them. I'm sure we all know what it's like when working with someone not liked. Even so, every message needs to be genuine. I'm not one for delivering fluffed up, long drawn out padded generalised messages that could apply to not one, but to anyone and everyone. I dive in with facts. I'm not a flower arranger, so don't expect a bouquet when having a reading with me - unless of course the flowers are a gift from Spirit. And it's definitely not a good idea coming to see me if you don't want to know or hear the truth. Unlike the living, there's something very special about deceased souls in that they never have a reason to deliver bullshit! I only wish I could say the same about some of the living!

The characteristics and personality of a deceased loved one communicating are very important, and as a Medium I do try to describe these traits the best way I can. It can get really amusing at times, to say the least. Like the time when a really fun-loving deceased soul with a naughty but nice sense of humour was connecting to my client, Georgia. He was saying how he was a 'flirt for the skirts.' He made us laugh the whole time he was present. As I was exchanging information between the deceased soul and Georgia, I suddenly felt my chair, a wooden rocker, start to tip over to the right. It all happened in slow-motion and despite wanting to try to save myself, there was nothing I could do. I landed on the floor sunny side up next to the Spirit who had pulled me over. All I could do was laugh with Georgia, who looked shocked, in an amusing sort of way. I didn't mind telling her loved one how naughty he was. He was showing us how he could still flirt. Nice bit of evidence, even if it was at my expense.

In spite of these funny moments, not everyone is welcome who visits. Unfortunately, we can't all pick and choose who wants to visit us either, that's not how it works. The door to the Spirit world is open to ALL, irrespective of who is wanted, or not. There are many unwelcome deceased souls I have had to deal with and send back. Apologies sometimes come too late for clients. Being dead and apologizing for all their wrong-doings just doesn't mean as much as it once should have. Irrespective of late apologies, an apology can also be gratefully received, if the client is willing enough to accept one.

There are times, too, during a home visitation when Spirit try to get my attention. They can do this by flickering with my house lights, which happens almost on a daily basis. It's not unusual for my electrics to malfunction. In fact, it's quite common for any of my electrical items to malfunction or die a sudden death.

I still laugh to myself as I remember one time when I had to go out to a seminar for the whole day. I can't tell you how someone over there must have been very pissed with me going out for so long. Anyway, when I returned home my Hubby couldn't wait to tell me all about his day and how he had to change three light bulbs. There were two outside the house that needed replacing and one inside. All had blown simultaneously. Even though I had to laugh, Hubby, bless him, was not amused.

Signs from Spirit can play an important part of their communication with us. So, one sign I am particularly aware of and pay attention to is the smell of death. I get this whenever someone has just died - or is about to make their transition to the Spirit World. Whenever I get a putrid odour surround me I know it is usually going to be connected to someone known to me, or to a visiting client. The smell of death is one I can't even begin to describe. I just know it's not a nice smell. It's also one you cannot ever forget. The smell of death will always remind me of the night my own sister died.

I get to meet a lot of people in my work, and obviously I get to meet a lot of deceased souls, too. Night times are really good for visitations and meeting people from the Other Side. This is because the atmospheric conditions make it a lot easier for deceased souls to exchange their energy between both worlds. It's easier for me to also hear the whispering of Spirit's chattering.

Spirit can be so busy in my bedroom at night, I often see their shadows pacing backwards and forwards around my bed. They probably pace up and down around your bed too, but unlike me, you may not be aware of them. Nothing to worry about, then, really, because if you don't know they are there, their presence (smile) won't bother you!

During Spiritual visitations, my bedside reading lamp may flicker, just for good measure. I've had many experimental playful conversations with the lamp. I've had conversations that have led to two flashes for yes, or one for no. Depending on which way round they want to play. Sounds totally insane, I know, but then I don't live in a 'normal' world, I live in 'two worlds.' However, should I get too crowded with the Spirit visitations, I visualise a column of heavenly divine light in the middle of the room. I then ask all my visitors to step into this vision of light and return back to Heaven and their 'home', the Spirit World. If I don't do this, I can feel exhausted as Spirit can drain energy from me, and from us, too.

Night times can be the best for me as I can relax, in a funny sort of way. I may not sleep too well, but then, I have never been a good sleeper. Instead, often listening to the radio. I use ear plugs too so I don't wake Hubby if he's home. I always listen to talk shows because I enjoy the frequent crazy conversations between the presenter and the caller. And, of course, a talk show wouldn't be the same without a bit of Spiritual intervention. So, whenever there's an opportunity for Spirit to join in the conversations, they will. Even if I can't see them, I can at least hear them.

Spirit themselves can become the real callers during a radio chat show. The voice of Spirit, not the presenter or the caller, will turn into a drawl and become loud, or their words are said very quickly. There is a distinct difference in each voice, especially Spirits voice. If I don't acknowledge the voice, then I always hear a sigh. I sigh. Sometimes I hear a voice say, "Carole!" and I'd have to reply saying, "Go to sleep!" There was also a time I would jump out of my bed and run out of the bedroom when I heard my name being called, as you do. But now, when I hear my name whispered to me, I remind myself how blessed I am in being watched over, whether I know who it is or not. Now, when I need to sleep, I just tell any Spirit visitors to go home. I treat Spirit visitors the same way I would treat everyone else – like they were physically here. I have to have boundaries too.

I love everything about working with the energy of Spirit. And, working as a professional full-time Psychic Medium, I have no shortage of clients as my diary is always full. Every day, people come to *me*, people ask *me* to help *them*. Spirit souls reach out and connect to *me* every day, not the other way around. I never prey on anyone, and I am a firm believer in that people will come to me if they are meant to. That's how it works, how it should work, and how I work.

Chapter 8
Physical Mediumship

I've been prodded and poked about more times than I would have liked or loved. I've had x-rays to find out the causes of symptoms from the pains I have endured. Frustratingly enough, not every pain or condition I have experienced has been medically and adequately resolved - or resolved at all. Many painful symptoms have remained a mystery, not just to me, but to the medical consultants who have had the tireless task of investigating me.

One of my hospital referrals was for a pain I had been experiencing in my right lung. This examination showed a slight small shadow, but thankfully was nothing serious. However, I do work with a lot of deceased souls who have suffered breathing difficulties and lung conditions. These conditions I have referred to during many readings and conversations because I have been able to feel the pain.

Arthritis was another condition I experienced in my hands. This pain led me to have three different forms of tests in two different hospitals, but nothing could be found. Nor could I get an explanation as to what the cause of the pain was. I have clients whose deceased relatives referenced arthritis during readings and conversations too.

I also had a lump that kept appearing under my right armpit and to the side of my breast. Despite many exams and scans, again, nothing was found, and no logical explanation could be given. I have worked with deceased women who had breast cancer and would refer to this condition during a reading through the conversation we were having. I've been left feeling really exasperated when no cause to my pains could be explained. Yet, I couldn't let every pain I endured bother me.

I am a Physical Medium. So, all of the above pains and conditions I can feel and make a reference to whenever I am working with a client or demonstrating mediumship. I am compelled to explain any physical pain I feel during a reading. I have to, its evidence. And, it's an unexplained ability I actually have. It's a pain or condition that can relate to a deceased soul's cause of death or condition they experienced.

I also have the ability to experience a pain my client, or someone connected to them has experienced or is experiencing. The deceased soul with me will reference the pain. When they reference someone else's pain apart from their own, it's their way of saying they know about that pain. It's their way of saying they have been giving healing to that person and on their pain. There are times when a client isn't even aware of a pain or condition someone they know is experiencing, until the deceased soul brings it up in a reading. A reference is made to conditions because they don't want their family or friend to suffer through their pain, especially as they may have suffered themselves before crossing over. Reaching out and helping loved ones heal is their way of doing their bit.

Sometimes I can get an ache or a pain for no reason at all. I know, it is a bit weird how I can physically feel a pain belonging to someone who is dead, much less alive, too. Don't ask me to explain how this is possible because I don't have an answer. There was a time, however, when I would wonder if the pains I were experiencing were actually mine. It also took a long time for me to realise how some of the pain I experienced didn't belong to me.

Many of the symptoms I have experienced and continue to experience are connected to the deceased souls I channel. Even down to IBD (Irritable Bowel Disease). I have channelled many deceased loved ones who have had this condition, or sadly, bowel cancer. IBD and colitis is a symptom I can genuinely claim as mine. It's something I've had the displeasure of enduring for over twelve years. It literally is a shitty condition to have! It genuinely is a life-changing condition to live with. It's often also difficult to diagnose.

Going back to when I was first diagnosed with Collagenous Colitis, it was when I was doing an investigation for The Royal Navy at Davenport Naval docks in Plymouth. I was meant to be there with my team for the weekend investigating a few haunted locations. I had felt a little unwell before the investigation but felt even worse during it. I had an over-active bowel. I had to leave the team and head home. Hubby took me straight to hospital. It was so fortunate he had come with me on the investigation as it was not something he would usually do. But given the distance, I wouldn't drive that far. Not that I was driving at the time as I was suffering anxiety attacks brought on by heavy road traffic with stupid drivers. Thankfully, Hubby doesn't interfere with my work, but he does support me.

When we arrived at the hospital the doctor accused me of deliberately making myself sick. He told me I was anorexic. I wasn't, although I had lost a lot of weight. I was down to six stone when once I weighed in at seven and a half stone. I would be wearing adult nappies because everything I ate went straight through me. I needed help, not insults. I got the doctor to discharge me before I discharged myself. I went back to the private consultant I was already under with BUPA (British United Provident Association). Fortunately, my employer had a Health scheme going with this medical insurance company that I contributed to. Because of this, I was able to have further investigations straight away. My consultant checked me back into the same private hospital, he knew my history and I knew he would get to the 'bottom' of it ... so to speak!

When I was in theatre being prepped, I asked my Healing Guides to step forward. I asked them to help my consulting doctor to find the cause of the problem. I couldn't live life physically and literally shitting myself. I spent a few nights in hospital waiting for the results of blood tests and biopsies.

My nights at the hospital weren't wasted. The nurses kept me up for most of them talking about the deceased souls who walk their wards. I didn't mind chatting to the nurses, or about the deceased lady I described to them who visited me during the night. The nurses found my conversations interesting. The chatter took my mind off worrying about me. Besides, I was happy, we were talking about my work, so I really didn't mind.

Keeping the staff occupied was something my consultant would mention to me often, and, with a smile on his face. I don't think he knew what to make of me. However, he did have a sense of humour as he got to calling me 'Mystic Meg!' Anyhow, this hospital stay was different. The Consultant thankfully did find I had the rare bowel disease, Collagenous Colitis, a lifetime condition I would have to manage and get used to. My Spirit Guides had helped this time because I had asked for their help, unlike the last stay when the investigations had proved futile.

At the time of writing this chapter, and about twelve years since my initial diagnosis, I have just returned from a follow-up at another hospital where I underwent a colonoscopy. I had experienced another gastric flare-up. However, it was good news as the procedure went well. Butt, from what I recall, it didn't feel like that at the time. I found myself actually screaming during the procedure whilst having a camera shoved up my bottom! And, despite being given a relaxant through a drip, it didn't work. It hurt like hell and I screamed like hell – yet is was a necessary procedure.

When the results came back, I was so pleased to learn there was nothing to indicate any form of cancer or disease. That was good news at not having cancer, but the disease left me baffled. Having had IBD all these years it was now gone. It had done a disappearing act. That should have been good news for me, right? Of course, but at the same time, I didn't believe it to be possible. I knew my IBD hadn't gone away because the evidence was still evident. My frequent trips to the loo were not for pleasure, that I do know. So, no, it hasn't gone away. We can all become 'experts' of our own body. I am still under the hospital and hope on my next appointment I can really get to the 'bottom' of things ... as you do!

However, being a Physical Medium means I can go through a whole day with a headache, stomach ache, feeling hot, cold, dizzy and more. I can feel and experience symptoms of pain that I can't explain. I can also feel miserable and moody, or 'lovely jubbly' and jolly for no logical reason. If there was a machine for a symptom checker, I would probably get a lot of use out of it, and I would probably break it, too.

Sometimes I know if a pain symptom doesn't belong to me, but to a deceased soul. In most cases, if I know it's not my own pain, I will tell the Spirit hanging out with me to take it away. This is because I cannot help until I can connect to the person or the client who is coming for their reading. It doesn't happen too often, thankfully. Nonetheless, I can't go around all day experiencing pain because I'm waiting for my clients to arrive. That just wouldn't do.

If during a reading I get a physical pain, I will ask my client if they understand the pain. I may also have to describe this condition a deceased soul is making a reference to. Whenever evidence of pain is given it can often be quite emotional and tearful because it's evidence of a deceased souls suffering. It can also be a sad reminder for not just the deceased soul, but for my client too.

Also, as a Physical Medium I can feel the type of ending connected to a person who took their own life to suicide. One symptom I can get with a suicide soul is when I feel a pain that goes across the front of my neck. I may feel a strangling sensation under my throat. As horrible and tragic as it sounds, I will also hear the sound of the back of my neck snap which always sends shivers down my spine. That pain is my sign from Spirit connected to a soul who hung themselves. Sadly, people can take their life through suicide because they can no longer cope. But not all suicide victims will want to re-live the way they took their life. It's too painful a reminder for them.

I remember doing a reading for a client where I had two male suicide souls visit. One, from the evidence he gave had hung himself. But I still had to find out what happened to the other deceased soul. It wasn't until the end of the reading I discovered just how he had passed. It was as the reading was finishing when I suddenly had a feeling of not being able to breathe. I had felt a rush of energy that filled my body from my feet to my head. I could actually feel myself drowning. I said to my client, "If I didn't know any better, I would say this other young man died through drowning." I was shocked and saddened when she said, "Yes, that's exactly how he passed."

I also remember the first time I had this drowning feeling. It was during a reading for a friend of a friend, Kelsey. She had been a little shocked when I mentioned a man visiting her. He gave a lot of accurate information relevant to her and her family. She wasn't expecting him. He was her uncle. I remember as I was communicating with him how I felt an energy rushing from my feet up above my head. It made me feel heavy. He made me feel like I was suffocating.

With a sadness in my heart, I realised then that this man had drowned. I could see the images of him floating on top of water. He was fully clothed. Once the shock of what I was experiencing and seeing subsided, I said to Kelsey, "He shows himself in the water, but he's not alive." I could see her face drain of colour as I asked her, "Does that make sense to you?" She nodded confirming this to be true. I continued to tell her how he was saying, "It wasn't my fault." Kelsey was shaken as she said, "He was murdered, then his body was taken to the river and dumped!" Words failed me. Who could do such an evil thing to another human being?

Sadly, I have had quite a lot of clients, many now good friends, come to me who have lost loved ones through the most gruesome of murders. The most prolific and horrific feeling I have experienced many times is being stabbed. The feeling of a blade penetrating through my skin is excruciating.

There are deceased souls who have been gruesomely stabbed multiple times. They didn't deserve that.

A life and soul taken by a blade is such a heinous, cowardly and senseless crime. For what purpose? And 'why?' Those affected by losing a loved one to a knife crime will never understand why, myself included. No one wants a war of knife crime on their streets. Yet, it is a war that is out there on our streets and out of control. The punishment for anyone who takes a life will never be adequate enough.

Regrettably, there have been quite a few of my clients who have lost someone they love to knife crime. There have been quite a few high-profile reports in the media of murdered deceased souls connected to many of my clients. Murders that have been on national and international television, newspapers, radio and the internet. Murders that should not have even happened. It didn't make the person who took a life famous, it made the victim famous, but sadly, for all the wrong reasons.

I have many clients, mostly parents and siblings, come to see me who have lost someone to murder. They come to see me in the hope of connecting to their loved one taken by the hands of another. Often, a child murdered by another child. They come to try to fill that void they are experiencing and missing in their life. Sadly, families on both the victim and perpetrators side of a heinous crime themselves become victims too. Yet, the only way I can bring a loved one back is through their loved one's memories from the grave. If this is all a client can have, and all I can give, then I pray to God I can give it. I know how a visitation and conversation may bring peace of mind to those who have lost a loved one and victim to murder.

Sadly, there was one client, Jasmine, came to me for a reading who was an exceptionally brave lady. The *visitation and conversation* from her loved one made the reading quite difficult. I never expected to see or hear what I had. I have learned not to expect anything, but instead be prepared for everything in readings and the conversations I have between two worlds.

Up until seeing Jasmine, I could not recall having experienced one of the most excruciating feelings of pain I had ever endured. Behind the intense pain, I was shocked and moved when I found myself having a conversation with a young female Spirit. As I felt her energy come close to me I almost wanted to scream out. My head hurt as I felt a sharp object cut through the top of my head. The pain that went through me was unbearable. Not in a million years could I mention the pain to Jasmine. This was not the type of pain I could ever mention to any client. It would be too devastating for them to know how much their loved one had suffered.

The visitation was from Jasmine's sister. She had been murdered. Jasmine wouldn't need to hear how her sister suffered. God Bless her and her family. It was a senseless murder and loss of life for a lovely young lady, sister, daughter and beautiful mother. I can never be prepared for any murder victim who visits. Neither can anyone be prepared to hear and relive how their loved one's life had been taken. No one can prepare themselves to hear about the pain and suffering their loved one experienced at the time of their death.

There are also people who take their life through drug abuse or overdose. This is another pain I can physically feel. The pain starts once the needle pierces my skin and I get the feeling of disorientation. Or, I am shown a bottle of tablets laying by the soul's side and feel physically sick and lethargic. The reaction I feel from overdosing is once again evidence. I can get this feeling, too, when someone living has been for a blood test, but without the feeling of being disorientated.

Besides all the physical symptoms from the suicides I experience, I also feel the pain from souls who have crossed through accidental death. Often too, whenever someone has been hit on impact, I will get a feeling of being knocked back, knocked over, or slammed against something - feelings that can relate to being run over or hit hard by a train or vehicle. Each loss is equally difficult to deal with and each pain is equally different.

I also know if someone was a heavy drinker, I may feel a little tipsy. If not quite pissed, actually! I will feel unsteady on my feet and smell the distinct odour of alcohol. Many souls who drank a lot can be quite amusing to work with. As one can imagine. Yet, not all these souls who pass to drink related problems are jovial. Many drunk heavily for what would be in their words a 'good reason.' Some souls have been driven to death and suicide through drink.

There are also the smokers who visit during a reading. Their condition is easily identifiable through the sudden cough I develop. I may also feel a pain in my chest or back where infection or disease spread to the lungs. Heavy smokers are the worst, especially when they continue their habit in the afterlife and blow smoke in my face! I'm a reformed smoker of many years.

Because there are so many physical conditions we can experience leading up to our death, I can experience pain as a Physical Medium through a multitude of conditions. Every symptom, or condition we experience will have a pain attached to it. And, in my work, I may feel or take on that pain or condition.

In sharing all of these experiences, anyone who asks me about their own health problems I advise to go see a doctor. I'm not a doctor, I'm a Psychic Medium - I just tell you what is already known, and what Spirit know. It's totally understandable how we don't like going to see our doctor. I know I don't like going myself, not because I'm afraid, but because I can never be too sure if they really know or understand any of the causes of the pains I experience. However, if I can really save a life by using my 'gift' of course I will. I will tell anyone go and get yourself to the doctors.

It's so ironic how we try to stay away from our doctor, but happy to tell everyone else to go. We stay away, ourselves, mostly out of fear. And because of what may be told to us. Men are the worst in going to see their doctor. But the best piece of advice I, and deceased souls can give, is to never avoid, delay or put off seeing a doctor. One visit could be the start of saving your life. Timing is everything, but means nothing if you're too late, or too dead! Getting to spend more time with your family because you made that right decision to get looked at and treated is truly worth it.

Chapter 9
When Heaven Calls

Funerals aren't very nice. We are all going to have one of our own, if we are lucky that is. Not everyone gets to have an end of life service. Funerals are that final goodbye we'd rather not say to someone we loved or were fond of. We'd much rather instead continue to have the person who has reached the end of their physical life alive and kicking, and very much around us.

Letting go of someone we love is very hard for anyone. Yet, funerals are a special celebration of a person's life. It's an opportunity and a time to reflect how you were part of that person's journey. It's a place you can go to pay respects to the person you will no longer be seeing, kissing or hugging. It's an opportunity for you to show how much they meant to you.

When I lost two lovely school friends in Debbie and Graham who were the same age as me. I was more than sad. They had died within a few years of one another. I was blessed to have been part of their journey as a friend. I was blessed to have had the honour and privilege of attending .their funerals. I had the honour of celebrating their lives amongst their family and other friends who turned up at the church to give them a good send-off.

At each funeral both of them let me know how they were present. I attended my friend Debbie's funeral first. I always had fond memories of growing up with Debbie - who lived just around the corner from me back then. I even took her to Manchester and the North of England when we were seventeen to meet some of my Dad's family. We were quite young to be going away without parents, but we loved the adventure and excitement in the freedom we would experience. There were many pubs to crawl around in Tyldesley, and we didn't leave any out. It was a shame however since leaving school we had gone our separate ways and lost contact.

We had both worked at Brunel University. The University was a big place employing thousands of people. I'd often be surprised who I did meet working there. Regrettably, I didn't get to find out Debbie herself was employed there until a few months prior to her passing. It was only through a chance meeting on campus that we met up again. I couldn't believe it when I saw her getting off a bus. I couldn't wait to go over and talk to her.

Debbie and I arranged to meet at the campus café later that week. During our catch up, not once did Debbie mention there was anything wrong with her health. I had no reason to believe there was. I'm not sure she even knew she was sick. Debbie had been so happy telling me about her children and life. I told her about my life and my furry family. We spent a good hour fitting in as much as we could reminiscing about the past we had spent together. I didn't realise how that meeting would be the last time I would see my friend.

A short time after we had coffee together, I was totally shocked and saddened when I got the news of her passing through an email. The email that landed in my inbox at work had Debbie's name on it. It was advising the date of her funeral and that friends were welcome to attend. As I read the email, I remember how my heart sank. I thought there had been a mistake. I picked up the phone and called the person who sent the notification asking for more information. I was hoping and praying it wasn't Debbie. Sadly, it was. If only I had known. If only I hadn't had to work such long hours, I may have had an opportunity to see her again. If only … I hadn't let my job take over my life – which it had. If only I had made time for those who should have mattered. If only …

I went to Debbie's funeral and sat at the back on the seat closest to the aisle. I always made sure wherever I went I would be close to the door, just in case I needed to leg it to the loo. The service was beautiful and well attended. I recognised Debbie's Mum and some of her family, her brother and Kirsty, Debbie's sister. Her children and Grandchildren were also present. I could see their hearts breaking as they wept uncontrollably. I could feel a lump form at the back of my throat as I tried to hold back my own tears.

When the service was over the family turned to walk back up the aisle towards the exit door. Debbie's Mum, Yvonne, whom I hadn't seen in as many years looked straight at me. Her tears streamed down her ashen face. I wasn't sure if she recognised me at first as it had been so long, but she did. She placed her hand on my shoulder. I smiled at her as I acknowledged this gesture. I also noticed how I was the only person she made this gesture to. I knew this to be a sign from Debbie and I whispered a word of thanks to her. I knew she was walking beside her mum, I couldn't see her, but I knew she was there.

The second funeral of another school friend, Graham, was also memorable. The service was held in the same church as Debbie's. It was also the church my Mum and Dad married in. And, the same church where Hubby and I had our marriage vows blessed.

Graham's service was beautiful. There were many tears from his family, children, Grandchildren and friends. There was a lot of love and laughter too. Graham was well known locally and enjoyed life to the full. I remember the conversations we would have sitting next to one another at the hair dressers. He'd be having a short back and sides whilst I'd be having my roots dipped and dyed! Between us, we put the world to right.

Graham's time had also come too soon and now the vicar was talking about him. His life was being celebrated. People were smiling in amusement at some of the memories Graham left behind. According to the vicar it wasn't just pints he enjoyed – he liked the odd relaxing spiff too! Laughter rang out throughout the church. It certainly lifted the Spirits from all those who were there.

Again, I made a point of a seat at the end of the row and at the back closest to the aisle. As we were all stood singing to a hymn, I felt a weight on my left shoulder. I turned to see Graham standing next to me. He was smiling. His silly straw trilby hat perched lob-sided on top of his head. He loved that hat. Yet, somehow, he always managed to look good in it. He wore it well.

Graham looked just the way I remembered him. He looked just the way he wanted to be remembered. I smiled back at him and thanked him for the gesture telling him "You're OK" He replied, "Good turn-out Carole, chuffed with the horses and carriage, nice touch." He knew his family and friends had done him proud. The celebration of his life was everything he could have asked for. It was everything he deserved.

Even though I'm a Medium, I never work as a medium when I'm at a funeral. Although it does have a weird feeling that perhaps some people expect me to. I always feel like I'm being watched, by both the living and the dead. It's a strange feeling to be honest. People knowing how I talk to the dead and that's the reason everyone is gathered, to celebrate the life of someone who has died. Sometimes I feel I shouldn't be there because it seems inappropriate. But, I'm also a person too who needs to be there to pay my respects to the person I also knew too.

Heaven is going to call us. But it won't stop us from wondering how, when, where and why we will 'die.' Even so, let's face it, not one of us will want to know our due date any time soon. I certainly don't. I want to enjoy life while I can - so should you. Nonetheless, when our time is up nothing can stop the process of death from start to finish. However, let's not go through life waiting or wondering about our physical ending shall we. Instead, pray for, and appreciate each day we can breathe. Pray for each day we are blessed to be with those we love and cherish. Pray for the time you have now to enjoy being with your family and friends who matter to you.

Showing gratitude and being thankful for all that you have, and for those who are in your life today matters. Let's enjoy our earthly journey and help others to enjoy theirs. Let's not bestow sadness or heartache on others, but instead help them where help is wanted. Love them where love is needed. God only knows ... We are all human trying our best to survive.

Sad but true, it goes without saying, some of the worst memories a person can have is with their own family. I know from experience how families are the worst culprits for feuds between one another. Siblings can give up on one another far too quick. Some families never even heal from the feuds - until someone dies. And, there's always that one person in someone's family who will suddenly appear when death dawns to pay their respects.

Irrespective of a long-time feud with a brother, Father or mother figure who has just died. Suddenly, an appearance at the funeral makes it alright. We are talking about the very same person who didn't give a damn about their dad, mother, brother, sister, son or daughter etc. whilst alive and kicking. No departed soul should suddenly matter for anyone at a funeral who didn't matter before. Personally, I can't speak for everybody, but I wouldn't want anyone from my family at my funeral paying respects to me who shunned me. I wouldn't want anyone to pay respects to me just because I was dead. I hear it all the time with feuding families.

Nonetheless, despite what people think or how they acted, paying respects to someone they haven't seen for years, either before an imminent passing, or after, is not going to make everything right. Take for instance when I was doing a show, I had an elderly gentleman from the Spirit world step forward to reunite with a lady in the audience. The lady was his Granddaughter. He told her how his son, whom he hadn't seen for many years had turned up at his funeral, like nothing had happened. His son believed it was the least he could do was to be there for his dearly departed

Dad. The deceased man told his Granddaughter how he never mattered to his son when he was alive, so wondered why suddenly his death mattered now. He had a point.

To say the Grandfather was a little pissed about his son's actions was an understatement. He was very pissed. The Granddaughter confirmed there had been a lot of arguments about this and his son paying his last respects. She confirmed things needed to be said that were still on-going. I'm guessing his son may carry a great burden of regret for the rest of his life. He just wasn't there for his Dad. Regrets are memories – memories cannot be forgotten, nor sometimes ever forgiven. He could have seen his Dad when it mattered - but chose not to. *HE* made that choice, not his Dad. All that mattered to his Dad now was that he was at peace, at home, and in Heaven.

I know for some deceased souls their transition to the Spirit World couldn't come quick enough. Deceased souls through their messages have told me how they prayed, or even swore just to be released from the pain and suffering they were enduring in the physical body. I'm told by many deceased souls how checking into 'Heaven's Hotel' was smooth and made easy by family who had reunited with them. I'm often assured that any fear about death and dying no longer existed on arrival. For many departing souls, their last breath really was a beautiful blessing.

Anyway, it's good to know how we are never alone during the transition, not for one minute. It's good to know life is eternal and continues to exist in another dimension. It's a lovely feeling how a beautiful divine and Spiritual light will surround us during this transition. This beautiful celestial light is filled with a welcoming and unconditional love. You cannot feel it until you experience it and are part of it. But, of course, you have to die first.

Hannah, my guide has also described how the celestial light makes our soul feel as though it is walking on sunshine; walking from one floor to the next. Hannah also tells me how our experience in departing from the earthly life to a Heavenly life may also be similar to walking over a bridge, travelling through a tunnel, moving on an escalator, or climbing the steps to the golden gates. Any one of these experiences will get us there. There will also be a total feeling of love, endearment and enlightenment. Yet, no matter how many ways she describes the transition, it is always a beautiful one. Every one of these experiences is nothing to fear but something to embrace. That's why I want to tell you this.

On arrival to Heaven, each soul begins their own personal Spiritual healing through the power of the light. Heaven is a time for loving reunions and happy celebrations reminiscing of the past, the present and glimpsing into the future of those who have been left behind. Every soul has a mission and a goal in their new role as a discarnate Spirit soul. Unemployed they are not, there's always far too much to do.

No one tells us we may be alive and kicking one day and dead the next. Yet, death itself is a built-in justified fear, and something not any of us want anytime soon. We want to admire, love and keep our physical body the best way we can. We want to be with our family for as long as we can.

Yet, the older we get, the closer we are to Heaven. The older we get the more likely we are to think about death, dying and our place in Heaven. Our physical wellbeing, thoughts and way of thinking make us aware of how much time we may have left to enjoy life. How much time we have with our loved ones. How much time they have with us. There is so much to life we need to think about, but we don't, until it's too late.

People can convince themselves they are ill when they're not. People can think they are dying when they're not. A question I'm frequently asked oddly enough is 'When am I going to die, Carole?' You'd think people would not want to know their 'Due date' is coming. But, they do, especially if their time really is limited in their physical body.

I don't tell people how they are going to die, or when, of course I don't, why should I? I don't know. And, what would a person do with the information if I did know anyway? Health problems that are of concern are for doctors, not Mediums, and sadly not me. Telling someone when or how they will die is not for me. I've asked my guides not to give this information. But, if I can use my gift where it is given to help clarify a symptom and save a life, I will, of course I will.

I recall one client, who is of course now an ex-client who tried to get a due date out of me for her friend. Yes, really! Unfortunately for her, and of all the day's she chose to phone me, she couldn't have timed it any worse. Not that timing was anything to do with her lack of compassion. I had lost my Mum when she had called, I was in shock. My mind was not in the right place to do a reading, or to make a decision that shouldn't have been mine to make.

During the short conversation that took place, I told this woman how sorry I was about her friend, but I couldn't help her. I told her how I had just lost my Mum, but that didn't seem to matter to her. My words went over her head, she wasn't interested in my loss. What mattered to her was whether she should take the holiday she was planning before, or after her friend died.

I was astonished and upset as the woman became verbally abusive as she shouted down the phone to me. Rather rudely, she told me how she was taking her 'business' elsewhere. The phone went dead as she cut me off. I was really grateful she did because I wouldn't want to work with anyone like that. If a person matters more than a holiday to you, surely you would instinctively know what to do? due dates, are part of the 'unknown' for everyone. And, they will come.

My Spirit guide Hannah, together with deceased souls have given me some comforting information about death and dying to share with you here. I hope, like me, you have found the words to be wise, comforting and informative.

Whatever physical condition we have at the time of our passing, we always receive healing with the love of God (if you believe in a God) and Spirit. Whatever symptoms, or missing body parts we may not have been born with, without, or had removed along the way are regrown to make our Spirit whole again.

We can all look forward to the power of Heavenly healing we will receive beyond the pearly gates. No soul goes without the process of healing. Death itself is a healing process and a natural extension of an eternal life. Please, don't be afraid.

Chapter 10
Soul Helpers

I want you take knowledge in those you love who art in Heaven will come to meet and greet you. Those who come to meet and greet a newly departing soul are who I call *Soul Helpers*. They will offer love and comfort as the soul leaves the physical body. They will tell the dying person not to be afraid. The very essence of their love and presence will make the newly departing soul feel less afraid. The transitioning of the soul's journey will begin either before or during a visitation from the *Soul Helpers*.

After the transition, I can tell you how a deceased soul remembers everything that ever happened to them during their earthly journey. I can tell you because they may give me glimpses into their memories they want to remember. Glimpses that is evidence of their survival in the afterlife. They remember the people who made them happy, and those who made them sad. Some will forgive and forget, whilst others may not. Remember, what you do with your life is how you want to be remembered. Memories really do live on in Heaven. Your foot-prints reach all the way up that long and never-ending stair case. Footprints that can be re-traced.

Hannah, my Spirit Guide, has told me how we are never alone at the most important time of our life. A time when we are dying and transitioning. And, from what she tells me, I want you to know, just as we are surrounded by loved ones at the time of birth, so we are at the time of our death - if we are lucky, that is. Not everyone has the opportunity of a gathering of spiritual visitors before the physical soul transitions into a Spiritual soul, because not everyone has an opportunity to prepare for a transition.

Those who pass through sudden, or tragic circumstances will not have had the opportunity to have been surrounded by family and friends beforehand. Instead, their *Soul Helpers* will come straight away. No one gets left out. There will be someone there for each and every one of us when our time comes. We will all have *Soul Helpers* who step forward to assist in our transition when the time comes.

Soul Helpers are the ones who meet and greet us. They are going to be either a family member and/or a very good friend. They would have known us when they lived with us on the earth plane. There may even be one or more of our ancestors who meet and greet us too. Perhaps ancestors whom we never got a chance to meet, or to know. In this case, they would want to step forward for you as they see you as part of their genes and their blood line.

Time is of no essence with spirit or our ancestors. It doesn't matter how long ago they passed. The only thing that matters is how they never stop watching over their family, and relatives on the earth plain. This they see as part of their healing. They see themselves, and quite rightly so, as a member of their continued and extended Spiritual family. Because if they were still in the physical body, that's what they would be - family.

Other *Soul Helpers* to meet and greet us, of course, will be our own group of Spirit Guides and Guardian Angels. They wouldn't miss the celebration of a reunion taking place in Heaven for love nor money!

A Soul Helper will always be there to make sure that each and every one of us experience a smooth transition to the Spirit World. They make our passing as peaceful and fearless as it can be. Piece of cake, nothing to worry about. Millions have gone before us, and if **they** can make the transition, then so can the rest of us. We are going to transition anyway, whether we like it or not. There is no 'if' only 'when.'

My Dad, himself, had *Soul Helpers* when he was preparing to transition to the Spirit World following his battle with cancer. Yet, the more I recall of my visit with Dad when he was in hospital, the more I realise how he was being prepared. He was going to evolve. Re-living my Dad's dying moments was something I've tried to forget. It's an uncomfortable memory for me, especially as I had never sat with a dying person, much less one I loved who was my Father. It's also a memory I cannot erase. No one can ever erase a memory of being with someone you love during their last dying moments. I didn't want to remember my Dad dying. I wanted him to be alive and kicking. However, I'm glad to look back in a different way with fondness as I recall much more of what we spoke of. Parts of conversations I had blocked out, until now.

During my visits to the hospital and sitting with Dad I recall a conversation we had when he looked at me and asked, "Carole, do I know anyone up there? Is there anyone I know up there who will be there for me?" By 'up there' I knew he meant in Heaven. Nonetheless, Dad's question surprised me, especially as he didn't believe in all this stuff that I do. He was Catholic, he shouldn't believe, but I knew he did. I looked at Dad as I held his hand and told him truthfully, "Dad, you have nothing to fear. Your brothers and your sister, Kitty, will be there. You won't be on your own."

I could honestly feel the love filled with emotions pouring out of my heart as I spoke to Dad. It was a different kind of love that for the life of me I can't explain. And, the love that surround us at that moment was meant for both of us. It was love and comfort we were being embraced with by Dad's *Soul Helpers* and family. We were both going to lose one another. We hadn't much time left to have many more conversations - or to see one another again. Yet, the love I was feeling was strangely immensely healing, it was serene. It was hard to describe what I was feeling. I just knew it was coming from Spirit and the *Soul Helpers* whom had gathered around Dad's bed.

Sitting next to Dad and looking at him, I was trying very hard not to cry.

I needed to be strong for him. I needed to be strong because I knew how he couldn't, nor shouldn't be strong for me. Something he would definitely want to be as a Father figure, but in his mind he couldn't. I knew he was strong, he was dying, but he didn't have the strength to fight the disease and the cancer that had riddled his lungs and body. This alone made him very brave. I had to show the same bravery for him. Difficult. No one can possibly imagine such a moment until that moment of losing someone is one we, ourselves, experience.

As I sat looking at Dad's ashen and worried face, I could feel he was scared. I was scared for him. I was scared for me, I was losing my Dad. I wasn't going to get another. He was dying. Dying is one of the scariest feelings a person can ever feel in their lifetime. I don't even know if the fear is because of the knowledge of dying, or because of letting go of all the people you love and are leaving behind. It could be a bit of both. As of yet, I don't have an answer. Nonetheless, nothing can stop the dying process, or the fear, or more often than not, the comfort that comes with it.

With Dad's question, I had a nagging feeling he seemed to know just who *was* there. And, I had a feeling he may have already seen one or two of his deceased family visiting him from the Spirit World. I had a feeling he wanted to check with me he hadn't imagined who he saw. Dad was certainly of sound mind, that much I did know.

People in their dying moments often see someone they know at their bedside. Friends and clients alike often mention visitations told by their dying loved ones of people known to them. They will speak of people they have been happy to see and have conversations with during their final living moments. And, to be honest, I wouldn't dispute what they saw.

Despite his own religion and belief system, my Dad was talking about and sharing my belief system with me. A system he should not have believed in as a Catholic. There are many others of the same doctrine as Dad, who also know about my world yet unable to admit to it because of their religious beliefs or cultural upbringing. But the way I see it is: those who aren't allowed to admit their personal belief of a Spirit World will continue to be forced to live behind a veil. The belief of an afterlife and Spirit World could be a system they truly do believe in - yet forced to deny.

Many people feel there is no harm in believing in something other than what they are meant, or supposed to believe in. Because of religious and cultural beliefs, there is no true way to measure the amount of people who really do believe in an afterlife.

Nonetheless, for family or friends, sometimes, the thought of a familiar face visiting their transitioning person can be really comforting. I'm glad I have this belief because the alternative would be devastating for me. I wouldn't want to be alone. I wouldn't want to be on my own. I wouldn't want to know 'that's it' for me, or for someone I love. I wouldn't want an 'End of' because I know there is no 'End' - there are only new beginnings. There is always someone over there in Heaven always looking over me, looking over you, looking after us. Someone is always ready and waiting to for us - and to have a catch-up conversation with us.

Chapter 11
An Orthodox Gift

Spirituality and Spiritualism is an Orthodox Religion, as well as a sacred belief system to a huge population the world over. Much ignorance about Mediums and Mediumship can come through belief systems and religions. So, I want to tell you a little about mine, and the way I see it, and the hurdles I go through to demonstrate my belief.

I unequivocally and unquestionably believe we all survive death through our consciousness. I believe in an afterlife because I get evidence through my work every single day. Yet, even though Spiritualism is itself an Orthodox religion, I don't get involved in it as a religion. Neither do I do politics that can restrict how I should work, or how I should present myself. I'm a Spiritualist and a free Spirit with a belief system, and I want it to stay that way.

I understand how religion and belief systems are instilled in people from childhood, which could be responsible for systems that are followed all through life. Some children do not have the freedom of choosing their own religion or belief system. This choice is made for them by their parents, Grandparents and Grandparents before them.

I had a religion and belief system that was introduced to me as a child. I was sent to Sunday School to learn about Christianity at the Salvation Army. It was here I learned to play the recorder, tambourine, and tuba. I learned about Jesus Christ and God. I held the Bible in my hands and recited verses, but I didn't understand what I was reading. I couldn't relate to what it was about.

If you were to ask me now if I understood the Bible more than I did when I was a child, I'd have to say 'No' because the Bible was and still is foreign to me. It's not an easy read, either. I don't believe in it because there is no evidence in the here and now that *would* make me believe in it. That would present a problem if I was ever asked to swear on the Bible! I can swear … a lot … but not on the Bible.

The religion of 'Spiritualism' is actually recognised in the United Kingdom as Orthodox. But, unfairly, and unjustly I might add. The religion and beliefs of Spiritualism are continually discriminated against on a daily basis. It is also the only Orthodox Religion its advocates are asked to demonstrate and provide evidence of this belief system. Yet, this is a widespread belief practice not just amongst Mediums, but amongst those who also believe in an afterlife. People will make their own personal choice when it comes to belief systems, with or without a personal experience.

Anything connected to the paranormal, including visitations and evidence from the afterlife is an individual experience. Unless you have had an experience, no one will understand. I know people who have stayed at places and come face to face with an apparition (ghostly figure) floating around the room. I also know some people I speak with have witnessed an apparition of someone they know. Yet, they would not dispute what they saw. Perhaps those people were also total sceptics prior to seeing a ghost, but since having their experience, scepticism no longer supported that belief.

Even the Pope, who runs a very lucrative business, cannot provide evidence of everything within his Orthodox Religion. So, apart from Spiritualism, there are no other religions asked to provide evidence of something that has been witnessed, yet people believe in these systems that are as Orthodox as Spiritualism, and, without having any 'evidence!' Before I believe in other religions, I need evidence of what I'm being led to believe, and that isn't going to happen, nor can it. All religions have been created by man. They are what they are today, belief systems.

My parents separated when I was young, so I never felt a need to question our religion. I had assumed as we had gone to the Salvation Army we were all Christians anyway. I went through a good part of my life with the knowledge that all my family members were Christians. However, this was not so. On the day of my Father's funeral, I discovered he was, in fact, a Catholic. This discovery came as the priest was blessing my Father and throwing holy water over his coffin. My brothers and I sat in the front row of the chapel smiling as we looked at one another in surprise.

As we stepped outside the chapel after the service, I stood with my brothers who couldn't help but nervously laugh. I laughed too as we all asked one another, "OK, who knew Dad was Catholic?" Apparently, none of us knew. I told them that it didn't matter what religion he was, we were all going to meet up in the same afterlife, anyway. We all go to the same Spiritual place called 'Heaven.'

After Dad's funeral, I went straight home as I needed to ask Mum about Dad and his religion. I burst through the front door and into the lounge where Mum was sitting. I asked her, "Was Dad a Catholic?" Her reply came, "Yes, why?" I was half expecting her to tell me what a silly question to ask, but she didn't. Mum spoke no more of it. Of course, I accepted how it didn't matter what religion Dad was; he'd had a good send off, that's all that mattered. He was our Dad, it didn't matter what religion he was, and it didn't change him as a person.

Religion doesn't change a person - a person changes to suit a religion. Religion can be part of a person's job. A belief system can also be part of a person's job. It can be their life. Yet, I believe no matter what job you do you should be able to do it without being bullied.

In my job as a Medium, bullying and harassment in my place of work has become part of the job, when it shouldn't. According to UK Law, it's illegal to bully anyone in their place of work based on their religious belief system. Except, of course, if you are a Spiritualist, or a Medium, then the law doesn't apply. If it did, there wouldn't be individuals protesting and demonstrating outside theatres. This really does happen, and people really have done this when a Medium has attempted to conduct demonstrations of an afterlife through Spiritual communications.

Fortunately, people now actually do have a better understanding and knowledge of an afterlife. People have had their own evidence and experiences that have counted towards something they believe in as true.

With the repeal of the Witchcraft Act of 1735 in 2008, it actually did Spiritualism a small favour. It heightened public awareness and interest through all the publicity. Mediumship is certainly not any form of 'Witchcraft', nor anything hocus pocus. Whoever claimed Mediumship and talking to dead people to be a form of witchcraft is quite misunderstood and uneducated. Times have changed.

I've never met any Medium in my line of work who has cast a spell to speak to a dead person. However, I have met quite a few witches. Besides being a Medium where would I, between my shows, or readings, including public demonstrations, find time to cast a spell? Not to mention spending time with Hubby, looking after my furry family, doing the housework, shopping, then have time to grab a few chickens to make up a few concoctions that form part of a spell to summon up the dead? Neither would I have time to dance naked round a tree chanting verses relevant to witches and their spells. It simply wouldn't work for me.

I'm a modern Medium, not a Witch! This stuff with spells is for the real 'Witches.' Someone somewhere has clearly had too much 'Spirit' and mixed up the labels on the bottles because a Medium … isn't always a Witch. Neither would I be happy to be associated as one. My Curriculum Vitae simply wouldn't have 'Witch' in the title. Nor would it have knowledge or experience of any witchcraft. Times have changed, people have changed. We all have a right to represent who we want to be. A Witch is not someone associated with me. No offence to Witches, of course.

It's also interesting how Spiritualism is the only Orthodox religion repeatedly being repealed through parliamentary acts. Compared to other Orthodox systems, Spiritualism does seem to get repealed the most. Regrettably, the downside to the new Repeal Act, which is now under the Consumer Protection Act, has to acknowledge any form of 'Mediumship' demonstrations as 'entertainment' or 'scientific experiments.' Excuse me whilst I fart! Do other religions have to indicate this? No! Do other religions give evidence of what they preach? No!

Working as a professional Medium, and I am sure I'm not alone, I feel grossly insulted and offended to be demonstrating for the purpose of 'entertainment' because of some ridiculous and bias law. This law has been brought about because of a body of uneducated bureaucrats who can't explain the mechanics of an afterlife. Bureaucrats who don't want to recognise Spiritualism can make it quite difficult for people like me, and those with a belief system in Spiritualism to practice. This is purely based on their lack of knowledge, understanding and experience. It doesn't make sense that millions of people who have seen Spirit manifestations with their own eyes are ridiculed and questioned about what they have seen, or an experience they believed to have been Spiritual.

I am not an academic, therefore, I cannot demonstrate for the purpose of 'scientific experiments.' Who on earth thinks a Medium without a degree can? Most genuine Mediums have earned their own degree throughout the years of practicing spiritualism. Apart from being quite unfair, Spiritualism does not sit amongst other Orthodox religions that are treated equally. I will repeat, nor are ALL other religions asked to conduct their belief for the purpose of 'entertainment.' Am I missing something?

Even though I do 'entertain' when I am working, it's because I feel it can help members of my audience relax. It helps those who haven't been to see a Medium before. I bring humour into a message that would have been part of that soul's personality. For me, I entertain for the right reasons, not because some repealed law dictates that people shouldn't believe all this important stuff about life after death and the paranormal.

A Medium has to practice, in good faith, as an Orthodox system for the purpose of 'entertainment' under the umbrella of Spiritualism. I say it at my events and pre-readings, not because I want to, but because I have to in order to cover the law. You see, I'd hate to get arrested, dragged unceremoniously off to the local nick with my Tesco high heel stilettos scraping behind me along a tile laden floor, swearing as loud as I can. Then, having the added prospect of a criminal record hovering over my head for something Orthodox that is shared universally. This is an event waiting to happen, but of course, it never will. No one wants people taking to the streets burning effigies, now do they?

Mediums work at many public demonstrations where the event is often advertised and where you know the Medium will attempt to communicate with the dead. Many Spiritualists and believers will eagerly visit such an event. Many people will visit this event, too, who aren't of the same doctrine, of a different doctrine, or not of any doctrine.

People also often go along to the theatre or a show to see a Medium if not out of curiosity. Everyone has a choice in whether to see me or another Medium demonstrating mediumship and communicating with dead people. People can make their own mind up if it's something for them or not. No one forces anyone to be anywhere they don't want to be. Besides, I certainly don't don a head scarf, wear big gold dangly earrings and go out there with my crystal ball preying on the vulnerable. Spiritualists deserve more respect and credit.

People don't want politics for a religion, and religion shouldn't be made political, since religion is a freedom of choice. Besides, who has the right to decide, or question any individual's belief system? Who has the right to question what people should, or shouldn't believe? Who are we to question the results of scientific research? Perhaps we should? Since it all boils down to scientific evidence supporting evidence of an afterlife.

We all have ONE GOD and ONE SPIRIT WORLD in common, not a Monty Python Fucking Flying Circus there to entertain people because some Members of Parliament, leaders of other doctrines and academics don't believe in an afterlife. Let's not make a circus of GOD and OUR Spirit world we are ALL part of in our own right!

Unless the afterlife can be proved by scientific research it will continue in the minds of some, but not all, to not exist. Yet, it certainly does, but don't just take my word for it. I know there are millions of people out there who can support my claim.

Perhaps I have given you some thought-provoking examples of how, as a Spiritual Medium, I, like others, are forced to live life in a world of secularism and discrimination because of something that exists that cannot be proven scientifically, or otherwise, to everyone. The Bible cannot be proven, either, yet no one questions it. But I know for certain that you cannot possibly dismiss something you have or haven't been given personal evidence of ... FACT!

Spiritualism is an Orthodox Religion, belief system, and a personal choice enjoyed by an ever-increasing and evolving worldwide population. You either love it or you don't. Personally, I cannot see what's not to love. Spiritualism, Spiritualists, the SPIRIT WORLD and GOD is everything about LOVE.

Chapter 12
Earth Bound Souls

I have had the opportunity to meet with many deceased souls over the years who have remained Earth-bound. Many of these souls have remained through choice. Some, perhaps because they haven't walked into the Spiritual light that reveals itself as a guiding light when transitioning to Heaven and the Spirit World.

Spirit rescue, or rescuing a spirit is something that is much needed in some people's homes. Whenever a presence of a spirit, or energy can be seen or felt by occupants of a house then it's time for me to help out, if I am asked. Some spirits can be a nuisance and need to be moved on and moved out (the Spirit, not the occupants!)

I do feel it to be a duty of mine to help earthbound souls cross over. I want to help each spirit soul cross over the road into a well-lit light so they can reach home and their final destination. I do this by imagining a beautiful bright white light filling the room with a funnel reaching up to Heaven. I imagine the spirit soul stepping into the light and going home to reunite with other family members. The light we step into is constantly shining. The road we travel on through the light is permanently busy through the heavy traffic of other souls, all going the same way. I may call upon an Angel for help or ask my own Spirit Guide to assist.

A bright light or being shown the divine light for the purpose of crossing over is not for all Spirits. Not all discarnate souls want to be rescued. Through my years of experience too, I have learned that I cannot cross every deceased soul I meet over, it would be impossible, and because that choice does not belong to me, it belongs to the deceased Spirit soul. If my help is not required, then I don't interfere. And, just like us, we cannot be forced to go somewhere that we don't want to go.

However, there's usually a very good reason why crossing over for some deceased souls doesn't happen. Some of these reasons can range from wanting to make sure everything has been taken care of with people they have left behind, to attending a proud moment at a family gathering, to loving the home they lived in and not wanting to leave. If a deceased soul is attached to a person they cannot separate from, they won't want to leave. The list of reasons an earthbound Spirit soul remains is endless. Perhaps you, yourself, can think of a few good reasons as to why you or someone you love would want to remain earthbound?

Normally, an earthbound spirit is happy to stay where they are. They don't usually get in anyone's way either. Most of the time it's hard to tell if an earthbound is hanging out in your house anyway. Unless it's obvious. For some people though, they just know someone is with them. Some people too can sense they are not alone. Perhaps even been aware of someone living with them over a long period of time. Perhaps, too, they are comfortable with their visitor.

Chapter 13
Suicide Souls

Suicide is hard for anyone to talk about, including me as a Medium. But, sometimes I know that I have, and will continue to have conversations with those who have taken their own life. I will continue to have conversations for as long as conversations are needed.

Understanding the reasons as to why a deceased soul takes their life through suicide is something no one will understand. To be honest, I'm not sure the person who took their life would really understand the consequences of their actions, either. What I do know is that a soul who decides to take their own life made a decision that would not have been easy to make. Suicide is a decision and a vision that grows within a person that progresses over a period of time.

As a Medium, I have met many people who have been left heartbroken through a loved one, or a good friend who has taken their own life. These are the people who look for answers from me and the person they love. They hope I can help to not only heal their heartbreak, but more importantly, help to heal the soul they loved who felt the need to end their precious life.

As a Medium, it's only natural for people to ask me is if their loved one is happy. From my experience through the conversations with suicide souls, I know they are. I know because they tell me how they have been freed from the pain, suffering and torment they went through in their mind and body. For them, mostly, but not always, it was the right thing to do. Sadly, the suffering and torment experienced by the person who took their life was something not visible to others.

Suicide souls can experience sadness, too when they pass over. They are sad because they just didn't realise the extent of their actions. They didn't realise how much it would affect their family and those closest to them. Had they known the effect they left behind with those who loved them, things may have been different.

When people come to me to connect and communicate to a suicide victim, I know they want to pour out their heart and share their love with them. They want the person to know they did, and still do care. The reunion and feelings between my client, myself and their loved one is without doubt, always very emotional and always very sad. Yet, it's also a conversation that needs to take place. It's a *visitation and conversation* that is needed for both the deceased soul, and the loved one wanting and waiting to connect.

Sometimes for many, I know how they blame themselves and feel responsible they did nothing to help. This is often because they had no idea that the one person they loved was suffering in a deep and dark silence. Realistically, no one could have done more. And, 'I should have done more' is something I hear over and over again from those who have been left to pick up the pieces. More often than not, no one can do anything - because they are not meant to. It's the way it was supposed to be.

At this point, I can tell you that ALL suicide souls receive a lot of love and healing when they get to Heaven. If you, yourself, have lost someone you love, please be rest assured in knowing how your person will get to reunite with family members. All of whom will look after your loved one. They will be in safe hands – I promise you.

Thankfully, not all suicides are successful. There are attempted suicides that are a cry for help. Those are the ones who really do want to be rescued, and quite often are. Fortunately, and miraculously for some, being saved was meant to happen because their call for help arrived just in time to save them. There are also some people who will try again and again to take their life until one day they will eventually succeed.

I have learned through this work how many people commit suicide because of other people. I have heard and listened to many heart-breaking conversations of a suicide victim's difficult earthly life. I have been told by deceased souls, themselves, how suicide had been a way out due to excessive bullying experienced at school or at work. Perhaps other reasons were of other people, or maybe finances, drug addition, alcoholism, terminal illness, heartbreak, loss of another person, depression, or relationships, including family situations got too much for the soul. There is always a reason that seems to be a reason for a life to end. There should be NO reason for a person to end their life.

My twin brother walked out of my life with his wife after living with my husband and I for four years. It was soon after I published my very first book. Apparently to her, my book, together with my work as a Medium, the subject of ghosts and my son Simon, was 'a load of fucking old bollocks!' Well, in her mind, at least. I had no idea where all that nastiness came from – much less deserved it. If only she had read my story - she may have thought differently. If only she understood what I sacrificed to write that book over the six years it took me - maybe she would have embraced my accomplishment together with the love I had for her.

Anyway, when she and my brother walked out of my life, I felt like I couldn't face life without him. I'm still shocked and saddened at his decision to cut me out of his life. My letters, birthday cards (we share the same birthday) and Christmas cards to him always came back with 'Return to Sender.' If they didn't come back, I'm sure they ended up in the bin. If only I could understand what I did to deserve feeling this immense loss. Any one of them could have talked about it or told me what happened to cause them to leave. I know in my heart and mind it was my book. I know because she told me how my book had been left upstairs on the bed.

Did I have suicidal tendencies? Put it this way … I live each day grieving as though he was dead already. Out of my three brothers, he was the only one I had grown up with and mostly stayed connected to. My heart hurts when I wonder if he should pass before me and we didn't get to talk. I feel sad with each day that passes that he is not in my life. Yes, I feel dead to him. I am always grieving because I miss him so much, and for what? Because I accomplished publishing a book. A book I couldn't even celebrate, because my brother walked out of my life. I didn't want to celebrate.

Yet, this is my job, death and dying is part of it every single day. Why shouldn't I think of how it will be, and how I will feel when my brother passes? How will he feel should I pass before him? Will I matter then? Did I ever matter at all? I can relate to some suicide victims in wondering too if they themselves mattered to anyone they loved. If your family matters then embrace them and love them, tomorrow is never another day that is promised. Family often fall out over silly things and then live to regret they were never there at the end. All I'm saying is ... was causing the time lost and hurt for another family member really worth it?

For me, my life should have been to love my brother and for us to love one another, an opportunity now denied to me. I loved both my brother and his wife. Our home was their home. The tears stream down my face as I write about him. I think about him every day. He is alive, living somewhere unknown to me. I hope one day I will matter again, and the tears and heartache will stop. I have lost someone I love. Don't let this be you with a member of your family. Talk things through, that's the decent thing to do, especially when someone who loves you doesn't know what they did to suffer your loss.

I know how often suicide victims see no future happiness ahead of them. I know, too, how they see a life not worth living or being part of. I understand how suicide victims see nothing but sadness. Yet, without question, I also know how life is worth living.

I want anyone contemplating suicide to know there is always that ONE person who loves you dearly and who can help you. There is always someone who can help anyone get through any darkest moments. You only have to reach out to someone and know you matter to that someone. There is always a different way out of resolving life's problems than suicide.

I want you to know as you read this, that someone, somewhere connected to a person who has taken their life, will possibly at some point want to go to see a Medium. Someone, somewhere, will want to get answers and an understanding of 'why' if nothing else. Someone somewhere will want to know why someone they love can no longer be part of their life. I know not everyone will know why someone they knew and loved resorted to taking their life. But for many, seeing a Medium can provide answers that can help the healing process for both the person seeking clarity, as well as for the deceased soul who took their life.

I remember one client who came to me a few years ago, whose name I will refer to as 'Nick'. He was extremely unhappy with his life and circumstances going on. In his reading I used Tarot cards as well as Mediumship. Anyway, I had to stop the reading halfway through. The Spirit I was working with was telling me how Nick was pushed to the edge. Apparently, he was going to tip. He wanted to take his life. As I stopped the reading, I said to him, "You don't want to be here do you, darling?" At that moment he fell to pieces, tears streamed down his face. I remember how he looked up at me and said, "No, Carole, I don't." He had lost so much his heart was hurting. I truly felt his pain. I wanted to cry with him.

Sitting back in my chair and sighing I told Nick, "You have a beautiful family, but you have been hurt, your job's shit but you are a beautiful human being. Life does go on, this is a temporary hitch that you will come out of." I didn't tell Nick anything he didn't already know. So, I waited and watched before I repeated the words my Spirit Guide, Hannah, told me to tell him. I said, "Nick, it's come from Spirit how you are an Earth Angel darling, you are meant to be here because your purpose is to help people."

Nick's face transformed as I looked at him. I saw the emotions in his face change to one of hope. I continued, telling him, "Your time isn't done here, you will get through this feeling of being unloved, and you will find another who will love you unconditionally." I went on to tell Nick, "Your children need you, too." What seemed like an hour was only a matter of a minute as I waited for Nick to reply. He nodded. He was OK, so I continued with the reading and we laughed as much as we cried.

As Nick got up to leave, I remember looking at him, and him telling me, "Carole, I was going to take my life tomorrow, but coming here talking to you has changed that. Thank you." I stood up and gave him a big hug. Then, for some obscure reason, I said, "Mind you don't have to pick yourself up off the floor." Why I said that I had no idea. I gave Nick a hug and told him to come back whenever he needed to. I wanted to be there for him through his sadness and pain. I wanted him to know there was someone there for him. I was going to be there for him.

It was a few weeks later I heard from Nick who couldn't thank me enough for his reading. He also added, "Carole, my brother died of a heart attack the day after the reading. I literally had to pick him up off the floor." Those words sent a shiver down my spine. Even though Nick had the broken heart, it was really his own brother who had died of a heart condition.

Nick knew it wasn't his time to die, and he certainly didn't want to take his own life anymore. When things like this happen, we don't know why they happen, they just do. The signs were there. Nick is in a loving relationship today and couldn't be happier. He also loves his purpose as an 'Earth Angel' - it gives him hope, and others, too.

Readings connected to suicide victims and their family is an experience that has been a huge learning curve for me. It has been part of my apprenticeship working as Medium and a huge responsibility. I have to make sure that the work I do between both worlds, I do it to the very best of my ability. I have been given a very special healing gift to use in both worlds. This in itself is a beautiful blessing.

Chapter 14
Knocking on Heavens Door

Everything we need to make the world a better place exists in Heaven, when a lot of it could just as well exist on Earth. Yet, there is only ONE way to get into Heaven, besides having the ability to knock on Heaven's door, which is on a technicality - you have to *die* first.

After the transition has been made by a deceased soul, my Spirit Guide, Hannah, has told me there is only ONE hotel we all get to go to. There is only ONE door that can be opened to receive our Soul. That door belongs to 'Heaven's Hotel.'

Between my sister and my Spirit Guide Hannah they have told me how Heaven and the Spirit World is the best place in the Universe. It has been described as the Rolls Royce of 'Disney World' only better. It's one BIG Hotel with unlimited rooms and a never-ending mass of space. It's very roomy. It's a place that is fun, relaxing, loving and accommodates lots of souls. At the same time, it receives lots of permanent residents as well as near death visitors. There are free unlimited excursions too, to visit our loved ones from anywhere in the world. Distance is not a problem, nor is parking. I'm assured there's lots to do with never a dull moment. It's a place where you would want to return to again, and again. It's a place where you really can live life to the full.

This place called Heaven is a place open to everyone 24/7. Thankfully without any time restrictions. It is also a place where you can either plan ahead and make a booking; or arrive unexpected. But, being afraid is not an emotion that is experienced. The ones already there that know you, they are the ones who will pull out all the stops to make your stay enjoyable. They are the ones who will make you comfortable for the duration.

I'm told how reservations at Heaven's Hotel have been pre-booked from birth for each and every one of us. We can ALL expect to use our reservation when we arrive in person at Heaven's Hotel, but, only when the time comes. Your reservations in Heaven will continue to be re-booked as many times as you choose – through your own number of reincarnations. There is no limit to the amount of reincarnations we can have. We have the choice to stay in Heaven or return and live another life.

Heaven is the only Hotel which has a lot of history connected to the past, present and future. This alone makes it good for business. The evidence speaks for itself in people continuously crossing over. There are never any complaints, either, because everyone is truly happy, so I'm led to believe by those already there.

The feedback from the moment of arrival is always positive. No one gets lost in finding Heaven, since there is only ONE direction …Up! The direction is to just follow the light that leads to the end of the tunnel with those who come to meet you, your *Soul Helpers*. They will be helping to guide you into the light as it embraces you. The light will carry you where you are meant to arrive, and your final destination.

The tunnel of light is one everyone talks about and is seen whenever you check in or check out of the Spirit World. Including when an NDE (Near-death experience) has occurred. Many people who have experienced an NDE often describe seeing a tunnel of pure bright white light. I've heard how this tunnel, at the moment of death, or during an NDE, can pull you towards the light. This light links us all to the tunnel of love. It links and leads us to the Spirit World. Those who don't get to reach the end of the tunnel will return back into their body. They will have had a glimpse and insight into how the Spirit World looks.

Some people claim to see people they know appear through the light. Some people have heard someone they know tell them, "Go back, it's not your time." More significantly, is how people will remember the experience and how it will make them feel for years to come. The tunnel of light changes the life of everyone who experiences it. It brings a new perspective of life and its importance to cherish it.

So many people have had life-changing experiences and have been influenced to lead a better, fulfilling life after seeing this beautiful, divine and empowering light. Some people have experienced how, at the end of the tunnel, and within this light, they have had an opportunity to glimpse a totally different beautiful world that awaits every one of us.

Heaven is this world; it's the most relevant destination frequently receiving visitors and talked about today, every day. It's a place where our life is celebrated by our family and our friends before we arrive. What's more, it's a beautiful REUNION we get to experience with so many familiar faces. We are blessed to be part of this world, and to share the love that is eternally endless. Knocking on Heaven's door is an experience we will all get to have.

Chapter 15
Dream Interpretation

I have visited the Spirit World many times, not just through the conversations when I am working with discarnate souls, but through my sister. She's called for me in a dream visitation to let me know and see for myself how happy she is. In my dream I found myself in her world, in her Heaven, and in her house made of glass with a huge glass roof. The warmth of the sun filled the room as I sat and drank tea with her. It was as though we had never been apart.

My sister took me into the garden where I saw my Mum's dog, a white poodle, Jenny, playfully dive in and out of the small lush vibrant green bushes. It was the purest whitest and cleanest dog I had ever seen. I have to say, she had never looked that clean when she was with us. Even the grass underneath my feet felt really soft. All the colours around me were absolutely stunning and amazingly beautiful.

After my trip with my sis, I was on my way home and aware of being driven in a car that didn't touch the surface of the road. Instead, it was gliding gently a few feet on top of the black tarmac. I noticed how the houses lined the clean streets, nothing was out of place. This journey I was experiencing was very special. As the car reached the veil between both our world's I remembered feeling immensely happy.

Since my visit with my sister was ending and I had to leave, I really didn't mind one bit. You see, we still had the same closeness we always had. Nothing had changed between us apart from our worlds. Whilst I truly miss my sister more than I could possibly miss anyone, I should have been kicking and screaming not to come back. I should have been hugging her so tight and screaming at her to keep me with her. But I wasn't. I knew I had to leave. More so, I was happy to leave.

After bringing me safely home, my sister told me to look after myself as she smiled and waved to me. I knew she had to return back to her home in Heaven. I knew I had to wake up from this beautiful dream my sister had invited me to share with her. It was one of those dreams you just didn't want to wake up from. It was a dream you would want to stay in ... forever.

The whole ambience of this trip to Heaven my sister took me on was simply beautiful and magical. It simply was ... Heaven. I can promise you there is absolutely nothing to fear, it's a totally different and beautiful way of life. It's a Spiritual way of life.

The thing about dreams is how we can have a really bad habit of misinterpreting information, no matter who or where it comes from. Dream messages are on top of my list when it comes to how they are interpreted by people. One dream can be interpreted differently a million times over and not accepted until the interpretation fits.

People really do live life by their dreams. People really can feel influenced by a dream, according to how it is interpreted. People can get in a right state of mind because of dreams they have had, and which have been interpreted incorrectly. So, please, be really careful how you interpret a dream, as not everything is the way you should see it.

An instance of a misinterpretation of a dream happened to a client of mine, Tracy, who had turned up for her appointment really stressed. She had told me how concerned she was at a dream she had. It was a dream about her dear departed mother. Anyway, in her dream, she had become alarmed and concerned at her mother's strange behaviour. She just didn't understand how her mother could behave in such a way. It just wasn't like her.

Tracy recalled how upset her mother made her feel. In her dream, no matter where she turned her mother kept slamming door's in her face. Well, Tracy took this as her mother being angry with her and not wanting to be close to her anymore. Tracy also told me how she used to feel her mother around her. However, since having the dream, she hadn't felt the closeness of her mother in the way she had felt her previously. She thought her mum didn't want to be with her anymore.

A lot of information about signs I get from my Spirit Guide, Hannah, so I asked her what was going on between Tracy and her mother. Hannah told me how Tracy had misinterpreted both her mother and the dream. The signs of slamming the doors shut was not her mother being angry, but her mother actually telling her daughter to stop what she was doing. Tracy was becoming more and more consumed by her negative thoughts and actions. Her mother was telling her to stop being so negative.

Tracy's mother also felt her daughter needed to re-evaluate issues going on in her life. She needed to learn to close doors that needed closing once and for all. Chapters of life that needed closing. Letting go of people, relationships and issues from the past needed to be closed. Tracy needed to move on and build a better future for herself and her family. That was the message she was trying to give her daughter.

During the course of the reading with Tracy, and the conversation we were having with her mother, it was clear how unhappy she was with many issues. I had mentioned in the reading to Tracy how she had been looking for love. I had mentioned to her how she had been on many unsuccessful and disheartening dates. It broke her mother's heart to see her daughter unable to find true love and her Knight in shining armour.

Tracy's mother knew how her daughter was hurting through the toll of past relationships. But she also knew how Tracy had been so desperate to find love, she dated anyone. Her daughter, my client, was also unhappy in her job and kept being passed over for promotion, despite putting in the effort and hours. Her mother saw her job as a dead end. She felt Tracy was working for the wrong people in the wrong company. Her mother wasn't shutting her out in her dream. It was quite the opposite, she was telling her daughter to find different places to go to meet new people. She was telling her to close the door on her job and look outside for other opportunities. Her mother was telling her to feel the love in her heart for the things that mattered that made her happy.

Tracy really needed to open new doors to start new beginnings if she wanted to find happiness and success. All she needed to do was close the doors that needed closing and make the changes to get to where she needed to be. She needed to make important life changes if she wanted to change her future.

Messages in dreams can teach us to pay attention to many things going on in our life. We can all learn something from them by the way we interpret them. So, if you feel someone you love has visited you in a dream, and you remember many of the details in the dream, write them down. Write about the journey you went through, whether negative or positive, and information that was given to you. Things may well prove to be relevant later on. If it is, know you heard it from Spirit first.

For those who can't communicate to deceased souls, I know how dreams are the next best thing to get messages across. So, hearing your name being called whilst you are sleeping is another way for loved ones in Heaven to communicate with you. People often tell me how they have been woken up in the middle of the night having heard their name called, only to find no one there. Then they question what they heard, despite hearing their name loud and clear. Yet, no matter how many times the memory of hearing their name being called is revisited, a person may not remember who was calling them, or why.

Having my own name being called has happened to me several times. And, every time I hear my name in dream, or semi-dream state I know it's someone from Heaven dropping by. I also like to thank the Soul, whomever it may be, taking time out to visit me – if I remember the dream that is.

Of course, there can be other reasons Spirit wake us up in the middle of the night; an emergency is one of them. I have heard how someone's loved one in Heaven has woken up their sibling because a fire had started downstairs. On another occasion, one client heard her recently deceased dog barking loud and clear only to find her room filling with smoke.

I know it's not a dream, but it can often feel like one whereby a deceased loved one visits someone at the moment of transitioning. Often, they can call out that person's name and wake that person up. They do this to let them know they have gone and are OK. A deceased loved one dropping by is a very special beautiful message in itself. It is also one that we are blessed to receive.

Please don't be disappointed if a dream or other kind of visitation doesn't happen for you. And please don't be disappointed if a relative visits someone else and not you. It doesn't mean they don't love you, of course they do. They just aren't able to visit every living relative at that moment. It may also mean the person they visited was more receptive to receiving the communication. Perhaps will be less frightened too, but maybe, to an extent, that person needed the visit. Embrace any visitation that may happen, chances are, you may not get another.

Chapter 16
Messages from Mum & Dad

Mum sent her own message to us the day of her funeral. It was one of those typical days for a funeral too. You know the type; dark, dismal and raining. The clouds were crowding the sky. People arrived at the house in dark suits, black frocks and polished shoes. Umbrellas hanging above their heads sheltering them from the rain. Florists had been dropping off and arranging flowers, wreaths and posies in the front garden most of the morning. It was a day I didn't want to come. We were saying our final 'Goodbye' to Mum.

I never realised just how much there was to do when someone died. I never realised how much I would get involved in parts of Mum's life following her death. Parts I knew nothing about. The house needed sorting, energy supplies needed cutting off. The telephone number needed to cease. Dentists, Doctors and Opticians needed to be notified. A Death certificate was needed. Friends of Mum's needed to be contacted to share the sad news. Everyone leaves a footprint of their journey. Mum had left a paper trail for me to close through the service's she used. And, and it was going to take time tracking down all the service providers she did use.

Today, people were invited to pay their last respects and share their love with Mum. I welcomed family and friends into the house as I stood on the doorstep. I looked at all the lovely flowers laid out on the lawn. They were beautiful, people had been so kind to Mum. All we needed was Mum. We were all waiting patiently for mother to arrive in her chariot. She would arrive in the Hurst that would draw up in front of her house, our house. Hubby and I lived there, too. She would be peacefully laying in her coffin that carried her. This would be her final farewell. It was Mum's last time to be with her family and friends. Today in my mind was her day, 'Mothers' day.

As I was standing in the hall waiting for Mum to come home, the telephone on the table next to me started ringing. It wasn't a normal ring but more of a tinkering. It sounded like someone was mucking about with it, which they weren't. I knew it was a sign. It was a sign from Mum telling me she was on her way home. And she was.

Now, Mum visits me turning up whenever she likes ... without knocking when walking through the door. I feel she is happy knowing how her life can continue in another world. I know Mum is pleased she can watch over her family anywhere at any time. She didn't stop being a Mum just because she died. Because she didn't. I know how her soul does live on, only in a different dimension.

Spirit souls never miss an opportunity to show us signs. And, one sign I will never forget was a very special gift Spirit sent me. It was when my Dad was getting ready to make the transition over to Heaven. He was dying from lung cancer. It was during his transition that I awoke one night to see a beautiful bouquet of flowers with red ribbons wrapped in cellophane. These flowers were floating in mid-air. I was in awe and amazed at the hundreds of signatures that speedily appeared one by one covering the tall dressing unit. I realised how these signatures were messages from Spirit souls. Family and friends in Heaven were gathering close for Dad.

Yet, I felt sad, as any daughter would, in knowing I was going to lose a parent. Dad died a few days later. I was privileged the Spirit World let me be part of their beautiful message they had sent to Dad. I felt privileged they did what they did for Dad and for me to see. It wasn't just my own evidence that I needed in knowing he would be OK. Spirit knew I needed evidence, too. He would be looked after. Dad would have been very proud.

It's true what they say, 'It never rains - but it pours'. Not only did Dad pass to the Spirit World just before Christmas but Hubby's Mother did, too. One week before Dad. Her passing came as a complete shock. We would never have expected her to go. As far as we were aware there was nothing wrong with her. Yet, she had suffered a sudden massive heart attack. Christmas time seems such a busy time for Heaven, Earth and the Angels. I'm sure like me, you too will always hear of someone who has lost someone either before, during or after Christmas.

I should have read the signs better that I received the night before my mother-in-law's passing. The sign was confirmation something was wrong. I was woken up from my sleep to see a glowing greenish coloured head and face on my wardrobe. The likeness was that akin to my Hubby's facial features, but without the green glow. Sounds crazy, I know, but I can't explain it any other way. So, I dismissed it, as you would. I was tired due to Dad being ill. I was silently grieving as I knew he wouldn't be in my world much longer. I didn't need Spirit playing games with me and went back to sleep.

We always think our parents are going to be here and be part of our lives forever. We always think our parents will stick around to see us grow up, and to see their Grandchildren grow up. Life can be so unfair because we don't get to choose who lives and who dies.

I truly believe our loved ones give us a sign when they have passed. My father-in-law did the same. Following a short illness with lung cancer, Hubby and I went to see him in the Chapel of Rest. He looked so peaceful. It was whilst we were standing next to Dad's coffin, we heard a voice say out loud, "You have reached your destination!" I think every hair on the back of my neck stood on end. Hubby and I looked at one another in shock before we burst out laughing. I remember thinking how apt! Hubby checked his pockets and realised the voice was coming from his mobile phone inside his coat pocket. The Sat-Nav we had used to listen to directions was still switched on. If ever there was an accurate message to be given this was one of them. My father-in-law really had reached his final destination.

Chapter 17
Fake News! Good News!

I always put Spirit souls in Heaven first, because they are my first priority. I help those in Heaven. I help them to heal. I look after my 'People' up there in the Spirit World through the relationships we form when I work. Those in Heaven are always in my thoughts and prayers. Mostly always on my mind too, whether I'm working with them or not.

My employment contract with 'The Spirit World' is constantly being upgraded to adjust to the changes that need making in my work, and my role as a Medium. I'm always changing as a person, and the changes have been quite significant since doing this work. I'm embracing and promoting the world's biggest platform ever in the 'Spirit World.'

It's taken a lot of sweat, tears and years to get to where I am right now. Yet, am happy to say my training as a Medium isn't temporary, it's with me for life. Mediumship is a part of me I can enjoy and share with other people. People can enjoy and embrace my life too, which is part of the Spirit World where it can be felt through the *visitations and conversations* enjoyed by both worlds.

I get how this work is not always easy, and, it can be quite difficult at times. However, I can talk the talk and walk the walk with Spirit. I can follow their conversations just as easily as I can walk the plank. You're probably having a laugh at my 'plank' and I laugh too, but not everyone will. It's not always funny getting words, or Spirits mixed up. I can be terribly dyslexic at times. So, if I get things wrong please don't correct me, I know what I mean. If it comes out wrong, and you know what I mean, then it's not a mistake on my part, it's a 'happening!' it is what it is.

I get terribly flustered and frustrated when I say something and it's the complete opposite. That's my life. Not everyone can write or speak correctly, nor is everyone pitch perfect and pretty. But everyone can be accepting of other people's flaws, and be kind in the process, too. True? I do struggle and blame myself when I get things wrong. Yet, one thing I do know is whenever I work, I know that my senses are working just fine. There's not much to fault there. It's just words and what order they go in I struggle with.

I am quite fortunate in that most people bear with me and believe in me. I have no time for do-gooders who want to use political correctness at every opportunity. Neither do I have time for ropes that can strangle us in a society where people can feel suffocated - or get easily offended.

There are people who want nothing more than to tell us all how we should work or live our life through them. People pressure can ruin many lives as the physical soul tries to keep up with the dynamics of people's expectations. The best piece of advice I can share from myself and those in Heaven is to live your life your way, not the way someone else wants you to live it. Be happy. Be creative with your life. Don't give a fuck what anyone else thinks. Chances are, they won't give the same about you! Stand in your own power and be your own ray of sunshine. But, always be kind, honest, respectful and helpful.

Many of us will end up being shared around on social media anyway. And, we all know how social media is one of the world's biggest public platforms. Everything we say and do is recorded or monitored by someone somewhere. We have no control what's put out there with our name on it. Furthermore, what is put out there can be nice and positive or it can be negative, nasty and destructive.

Information people put on the web can make us or break us. Each and every one of us using social media will be affected by someone's view about us. Be wise enough to mentally and emotionally reject anything that doesn't put you in a good light. Unfortunately, with today's technology, many of us tend to become a victim of this visible social and anti-social World Wide Web platform.

Many people rely on social media for business. I know I do. Many people have a job to do. Social media is very important when it comes to representing a person, or the job they do. Each and every one of us need to provide food on our table, clothes on our back and a roof over our head. Just like Jesus did, himself, a profit of predictions with healing abilities, allegedly. He was also apparently looked after by the people who believed in him. Perhaps Mediums and healers got their 'Gift' from him? Who knows! I see many similarities.

We need to understand and accept that not everything seen or read about is the truth. Anything and everything can be portrayed or edited to look like another person's truth. Not everything is real, yet everything can be made to look real. Not everyone is fake, yet people can be made to look fake. Many of us will be the 'star' in someone's social media drama. And, there are some who seem to want to make 'live' recordings that humiliate others - even if it kills the person they are humiliating. I know because I've been a target of editing and humiliation. Thankfully, I survived, my heart and soul survived because I knew the truth. Social media, sadly, can be very much an alternative ugly, unregulated platform for harassment and bullying. It is also a space and a place where suicidal tendencies can be created.

At one of my shows where I was demonstrating, I was fortunate to be able to stop a person recording me. The video could have ended up on social media, if that was the intention. It could have also put me in a bad light. Perhaps ruin my reputation as well, if people were gullible enough to believe the recording. However, being fair, it can happen at any show where I have given messages and where information may not be accepted. Neither myself or my audience will know why until it becomes apparent.

Anyway, at this one show I had started off so well with linking in with a deceased Father figure to a lovely lady sat at the back of the hall. The evidence had been going great until the lady started saying 'No.' She said 'No' a few times. I thought this wasn't right. I couldn't help but feel something was wrong. I always trust Spirit and the information they give. There was no point continuing because the link had been broken. A broken link can happen either by Spirit themselves, or intentionally by the person receiving the message. In this case the link was broken by both.

As I was giving this message, I became aware of a bright light directed towards my eye line. It wasn't Spirits light guiding me, it was worse. I saw a lady holding her mobile phone up above the heads of those sitting in front of her. She was aiming the phone towards me. The light was blinding me, it was off-putting. She was recording me. I'm sure she didn't realise just how bright the light was. So, I politely asked the lady to stop recording. I wanted her to stop recording not just because of the light in my eye, nor because of the few 'Nos' I was getting with the link I was trying to make, but because I had a feeling the lady I was connecting with didn't want to participate in receiving the message for some reason.

Apart from all the above and not liking my own voice on recordings, I have a duty to respect and protect the other people at shows who are receiving a message. They may not want their faces, or messages plastered all over the internet (something which is now illegal). Nonetheless, the conversation with the message I was having with the lady saying 'No' wasn't making sense to her receiving it, or to me giving it. Thankfully, Hannah, my Spirit Guide stepped in and said, "Carole, there's nothing wrong with the information you are receiving but you need to cut the link." I didn't need to be told twice, so I did. I thanked the lady for what she could take. I also reluctantly turned to apologise to the deceased gentleman standing next to me who had been giving the information and said, "Sorry darling, I can't help you anymore, thank you for trying though." I had to ask him to step back and go home, I could do no more for him, much to his dismay.

I was thanking Spirit, after Spirit, after Spirit. I was thanking each of them for their love and memories they had been sharing with their loved ones during the first half of the show. Irrespective of it looking like I got off to a bad start (which technically I didn't) with the first message.

During the break, the lady whom I first connected with approached me. Standing in front of me she said, "Carole, I'm so sorry, I want to apologise." I looked at her saying, "please don't apologise, it happens, I'm sorry you couldn't connect." She looked at me and said, "But I could, I'm with my husband and my son. We could take all of it, everything." I smiled at her saying, "I know you could, but I couldn't work with you anymore because you kept saying 'No' darling." Again, she apologised saying, "I was too embarrassed to continue because I didn't like the microphone, and my husband and son wouldn't take the microphone either." This is what stopped the message from being given. I thanked the lady as she validated all the names, dates and health conditions I had spoken of. It was such a shame she didn't work with her relative who had done so well for them.

However, for the sake of my reputation in front of the packed hall I needed her to validate the information I gave her as being correct. I wanted her to take the microphone after the break and tell everyone she could take the message. She refused. She wouldn't, nor couldn't. Neither could her family with her. I needed to let my audience know I wasn't making all this stuff up I had given her. So, instead, I asked if she would give me permission to confirm the message myself after the break to my audience. This she gladly agreed to.

Following the break, I stood back on the floor in front of my audience with a big smile on my face. I told them of the message I had tried to give to the lady at the back who was my first link. I told them how everything I gave to her could be accepted. After I had finished putting my reputation back in tact there was a huge round of applause and a lot of smiley faces. I searched the back of the hall to find the lady. I saw how she was smiling and nodding away quite happily. She was confirming I had been right in all the information I had given. Phew! I never doubted myself or Spirit.

With that all sorted, what I had forgotten to do was to tell the lady who had recorded me that the video was no longer relevant. It didn't record the bit where the lady confessed. Now, if the lady chooses, she can upload that video on line for the world to see. However, it would be fake. I never give permission for recordings because of this. And, because people can, and do edit video maliciously, as has happened with me before. And, because people often come to me either in the break or after the show with their confession. Yet, not everyone will know if a recording is fake or genuine - because not everyone will know the truth.

So, let's be careful in how much we are led to believe, and never let us judge a person by someone else's cover story, least of all someone else's 'Fake news!' whether it's in printed materials, film, on social media, the World Wide Web or on our TV screens. People will make you look how they want you to look. And, remember, one day, it could be you looking to defend your image, reputation, career, family, or something else.

Chapter 18
Messages from the Morgue

It's a complete myth that once we reach Heaven we cannot return to visit our loved ones straight away. I know this is not true. I know we can. We can do anything we want. The evidence I have received through numerous readings has dispelled this myth.

Because of this, I am going to give you evidence of how deceased souls have visited me from the morgue. The evidence through their own *visitations and conversations* tell their story. Their visitations demonstrate evidence of their ability to return instantaneously. There are no restrictions or universal laws that dictate our free-will in the Spirit World. There is no one to say when we can and can't come back to visit those we have left behind. We are in control of our own consciousness and free-will.

An example of how quickly a deceased soul returned happened when I was working in my office at the University. It was a visit I could have done without, given it had been an exceptionally busy day. I was up to my eyes working on a research funded project for the European Commission. The Project Commissioner from Brussels was visiting so we had a lot of preparation to do. Everything had to run smoothly.

All those, in the team, including myself involved in the project had dined with the Project Commissioner from Brussels. It was the night before I had the visitation. At the dinner table I was sat opposite the Commissioner and let him lead the conversation. I nearly fell off my bloody chair when he spoke about the paranormal and the haunted places he wished to visit. He told me he had a copy of my first book, 'The Living Spirit, One Woman's

Battle Amongst Ghosts, Spirits and The Living.' He also told me he enjoyed reading it. He laughed as he told me how he had to let go of it when his son asked to read it. Many European work colleagues spoke highly about me, my work and my published book. I just didn't realise how I would be known as high up as the Project Commissioner in Brussels!

Anyway, it was a busy day at the office and I had deadlines to meet. I had also closed my door to limit the amount of interruptions from members of staff. Normally, Spirit would never bother me during my day job and office hours. I always give specific instructions to them not to disturb me whilst I'm at work. However, I had received a text message from Emily, a friend of mine, and needed to reply. I had just finished pressing the send button when my office went a very icy cold. I felt cold. Out of nowhere appeared a man floating on a slab sitting upright. I really appreciated how he was visiting me fully clothed. I could see he was also quite tall. This visitation was definitely different, and I knew it wasn't going to be good.

I looked at him looking at me. It was safe to say we were both shocked. I knew nothing about him and had never met him. I hadn't got a clue who he was. He probably didn't know who I was either, or how he ended up in front of me and in my office. I can't explain that one either. I Just didn't know who he was connected to. All I knew was that he suddenly appeared following the text message I had answered and replied to from Emily. As it happened, Emily also worked in a funeral parlour. But I never thought for one moment I would get involved with her clients. I had no need - I had plenty of my own. But I did get involved.

The deceased man's actions were the same as those of a 'living' person who wanted to reach out. He needed help. Visitations from the morgue would become a normal day and way of life for me, as I was to find out. Yet, I needed to find out where this man came from. So, I had to put my thinking cap on. My first and only instinct was the funeral parlour. The place where Emily my friend worked. It was the only place that could have possibly linked me to him.

The only way I could find out who he was would be to ask him. So, I did. He was still floating around in front of my desk when I asked, "Hey, hello darling, who are you?" His face looked blank as he stared at me. I asked him, "Do you know what happened to you?" He was trying to talk but all he could manage was a mumble. I told him, "It's OK, I will try to help you, tell me what happened to you, please." He was looking around my office talking to himself and not making much sense. Then he turned to look at me saying, "I don't know, I had a sharp pain in my back and under my shoulder blades." He continued by saying, "I don't understand why people can't see or hear me, but you can." I took a deep breath before I told him, "I talk to dead people. I'm so sorry, but you are dead darling, something happened to you." I could see by the look on his face he wasn't happy. I didn't blame him either to be fair, as he was dead, but just didn't know it. He didn't respond.

I quickly texted my friend Emily and asked her "Have you got a gentleman staying with you in the Chapel of Rest today?" Her reply came back, "No." I was puzzled. I wanted to know who this man was. Feeling desperate, I texted my friend again asking her "Are you sure you haven't got a gentleman with you?" Again, her reply came back, "No". I was not only puzzled, I was also troubled. Why was he here with me if I couldn't connect him to anyone? The poor man was in shock at my telling him he was dead. All he could do was mumble.

I wanted to carry on with my work. I could ill afford any disruptions or distractions from this man, Spirit, or anyone else. I had to work. Nothing phases me with dead people. But I could see this deceased man was clearly distressed. I stopped what I was doing. I looked at him and told him, "I'm so sorry darling, there is nothing I can do for you here. I have no one to connect you to." His mouth moved but no sound came out. I watched as his energy and his whole being disintegrated and disappeared. He was gone.

Maybe he had already tried to get the attention of his family, but to no avail. I don't know. Not everyone can see Spirit. That I do know.

Learning to trust my gut feelings and listen to my psychic intuition is something I had got used to doing. My feelings and intuition told me the man was going to be connected to my friend's workplace at the funeral parlour. I was right with my instinct. A few days later my friend called me telling me of a gentleman I had asked about. He had arrived at the Chapel. His wife had visited the parlour to arrange his funeral. He had been in the morgue when he came to me.

Emily told me of the events that led up to the man's passing. Apparently, the lady's husband had mentioned to his wife a pain he had been experiencing. It was the same pain he had described to me between his shoulder blades. Emily told me how the man had asked his wife that very morning if he should go to A&E (Accident and Emergency) at the hospital. He asked her if he should go there or to his doctors. His wife had told him to wait and see if the pain went. Unfortunately, he collapsed later that day and an ambulance had to be called. Sadly, he died.

Through his wife's account of her husband's tragic passing to my friend, we learned how he passed with a heart attack. This started with the pain in his back and under his shoulder blades. He thought he would be OK. He knows, too, how his wife wasn't to know how serious his pain was, she can't be blamed. What seemed like something so minor turned out to be something very fatal.

There can always be too many 'If I did' or 'I should have done' scenarios that perhaps would not have helped in any given situation. Life is life. We have no knowledge of when it can end, only that it will. We should all know just how something can and will happen to any one of us at any time. Death and dying isn't just something that happens to other people.

Our loved ones will almost always inevitably find a way to connect and communicate. This wonderful deceased soul was able to connect to me through my friend, much to her astonishment, and mine. I feel sure he will try to contact his widowed wife, if he hasn't already done so. Through this experience I learned to identify the difference between a soul that has crossed over and a soul who is waiting (in the morgue) to cross over. The icy-coldness in the energy is vastly very different. The man was my very first experience of a visitor from the morgue, but he wasn't my last.

I had the same ice-cold feeling surround me when a client of mine, Val, came to see me for a reading. As I started the reading, I was aware of a Spirit energy standing close to me. I could see he would have been middle-aged before he passed. He announced himself as Pete. He also claimed to be Val's husband. He was quickly acknowledged by Val and the information we exchanged between one another was correct and accepted. I couldn't let his coldness or mine go without a mention. So, I mentioned to Val how icy cold he was. I also mentioned how he must have recently been deceased too. Val confirmed he had. And, she also confirmed how her Pete was still in the morgue.

In talking to Pete, he mentioned how he had passed very suddenly. He impressed upon me physically a condition of a heart attack. He also claimed how he didn't have time to sort out his life before his departure. I told Val what Pete had said and she confirmed it all to be true.

With the reading in full swing, Pete didn't hold back. For someone who had just died he was absolutely full of life as he shared his love with us. He certainly amazed me. Anyhow, I told Val, "He says he hasn't been gone two weeks." I watched as she nodded her head in agreement. She also confirmed how his funeral was taking place in another two weeks' time.

I felt Val was very brave coming to reunite with her husband so very soon after his passing. And as for Pete, well, he didn't hesitate in wanting to reunite with his wife, either. It was important for Val to receive evidence of her husband's survival in the afterlife, which she certainly got. Right down to the brand of the new sofas they had purchased prior to his passing. Pete was pleased to be back. He was still very much alive and kicking, albeit in a different world. The evidence in the conversation from Pete was comforting for both Val and her 'Pete.' They were both in good Spirits. This was demonstrated through the love and laughter that was shared between two very lovely loving souls.

Val didn't hesitate to come back to see me again a few weeks later, but not for herself. This visit was for Coral, a friend of hers. Coral had booked in for a reading but wanted Val to sit in with her. She was too nervous to sit by herself. The reading was going really well until Coral started saying, "No." That's when I knew something was wrong, so I stopped. Val looked at me laughing as she said, "That's my Pete, Carole!" We all laughed. How naughty was Pete! Coral didn't mind Pete butting in since her reading was almost finished, anyway. I guess Pete thought he would take another opportunity to let his wife know he was still watching over her. I could tell how he loved his wife very much.

Pete was very much loved, too. He really was a lovely soul who had really nice Spiritual energy. He made the rest of the *visitation and conversation* very light-hearted. His message was filled with more evidence and even more loving memories of his life with his wife. He was as 'happy as Larry'. I'm a poet and don't I know it! Pete, he could once again communicate with Val, who was over the moon with his visitation. Between them they had a lovely catch up conversation - for 'old time's sake'.

There was another lady and client who visited me, Karin. Tragically, her husband had been in a coma for many months. His brain had been starved of oxygen. His life-support machine was soon to be turned off. During the reading Karin's husband gave evidence it was him joining us. He told of many things connected to his wife and family. I remember fighting back tears as he told me the date his life-support machine was going to be switched off. I told Karin the date her husband had mentioned which she confirmed the date to be true.

It was a heart-breaking decision for the family. But Karin's husband had wanted to tell his wife and family it was the right thing to do for him. He was giving his approval and didn't want them to suffer any longer than he felt necessary. He wasn't going to come out of the coma. The injuries to his brain were too extensive. He told his wife he didn't want to suffer, either.

The message from Karin's husband comforted her and her family. It comforted her husband, too. This was his last chance to say 'Goodbye' to his wife and family through the message of many memories in the conversation we shared. He wanted them to know it really was OK. He was OK.

This message, for me, was really surreal. I had never given a message from someone who was in a coma. But since consciousness survives and can travel, I believe this is what happened. I believe Karin's husband's consciousness was with us at the time of her visit with me.

Science has proven that consciousness survives. With the permission from the next of kin, perhaps using a Medium to communicate with those who are in a coma is something that can be used for scientific research. Who knows? It's something worth considering that could prove helpful and could prove beneficial, not just to family's who wait for their loved one to come out of a coma, but beneficial to science, too.

It's not for me to say when someone should visit after losing a loved one. It's not for me to say how long someone should wait before a visit to me is needed. It may not be what you would do or your view either. But then, it's someone else's loss, not yours. Besides, it is a personal choice. From experience, connecting and communicating soon after a passing can be a happy reunion in both worlds. I like to think of deceased souls as not being alone soon after their passing. I like to think that someone they love will reach out to them and comfort them too.

Chapter 19
Psychic Fayres

I have mentioned the first Psychic Fayre I visited in my first book, "The Living Spirit, One Woman's Battle Amongst Ghosts, Spirits and The Living" but I feel it poignant to recap on how that experience gave me the courage and confidence I needed to sit behind a table as a Medium doing readings, myself. Like the other readers at the fayres, I, too, felt a need to share the loving memories with those who came to see me from those who had passed.

I remember the very first time walking into a hall at a local psychic fayre. I remember noticing the many boards displayed on each table across the hall strewn with big bold letters across them reading: 'Tarot Reader,' 'Clairvoyant', 'Your Future Told', 'Your Destiny?', 'As seen on TV', etc. The information displayed was endless. The people sitting behind the tables were of interest to me, and I wanted to know more.

Even though I wasn't a Medium back then, I was curious. I had always been curious of something. Quite what, I didn't really know. Yet, here I was looking and searching for someone I hoped I could have a conversation with. I wanted to learn about the type of work they were doing and what you had to do to get a table. I needed to know more about Spirit and Mediumship. I felt that was the part of me I needed to 'fix.'

I walked around the hall wondering who to go to when I was drawn to a Clairvoyant. She was an elderly lady, smart in appearance. She had an air about her I felt comfortable with. She looked totally down to earth. She didn't glam up her table, either, like the other Psychics and Mediums. Her table was almost bear. She didn't have much, but I somehow knew she would do, and I knew I had to see her. She began to tell me about my sister, Christine. I could feel my heart beat ten to the dozen as I was being given information this reader couldn't possibly know. She told me, "She said you're not ready, you need to learn." I knew what she meant. I also knew Christine guided me to Maureen and her table. I left with tears running down my face. I was happy. My sister knew I wanted to give messages, but she knew I wasn't ready. She was right, I wasn't. I knew dip shit.

However, there was something about what I had just heard in my reading that released something inside me. I felt very different. Something had happened to me I couldn't explain. I felt happy my sister knew I was going to be a Medium one day. She was going to help me. It felt good to hear how my sister was watching over me. Something I knew anyway, but it's always nice to hear it from other people. That reading I had changed my life. It was also the start of my developing Mediumship.

The help through the reading Maureen gave me was priceless. She was also someone whom I would like to thank from the bottom of my heart - if ever I find her again, that is. Maureen, although she doesn't know it, totally changed my life. I've found who I am supposed to be and I'm doing what I'm supposed to be doing.

It was many years later when I was able to have my own table at a Psychic Fayre. Just like I knew I would. I remember going out the door with my bags packed full of Tarot cards, brochures, table cloths and a banner. And, just like Maureen, my table too would be almost bare. I arrived at my first venue ready to rock. The evening went smoothly with every customer smiling and satisfied. I felt proud to have helped people. I felt humbled knowing how people would take away a memory of their reading with me. People were taking away a little piece of Heaven from someone they love. I know they would experience the same feeling as I had with Maureen. I wanted to help people in the same way Maureen years earlier had helped me.

Whenever I worked at a Psychic Fayre, I began to notice how Spirit Souls would gather around my table. They would wait for their person somewhere in the hall to come over to me and make their connection from the Spiritual realms. I also knew how I was just as genuine as those Psychic Mediums who were at the fayre I first attended.

I recall one fayre I was working at where I did a reading for an elderly lady. Her reading proved to be exceptionally moving. The lady was on holiday from America. Her relatives had been showing her around and bought her to the fayre. I had watched as she approached my table. I had noticed how she didn't hesitate as she sat straight down in front of me. She hadn't given any of the other readers a once over at all. Instead, she marched right over to me. It was like she knew where she was meant to be. Almost straight away she asked very softly, "Can I have a reading with you, please?" I smiled at her and said, "Yes, of course you can darling, please make yourself comfortable."

As soon as she asked about a reading, I felt the coldness of an energy step forward. Someone had drawn close to visit this lady. I could see he was an elderly gentleman. He also announced himself as her husband. I was happy for her as I said, "Darling, I have a gentleman here claiming to be your husband. He's not very tall" I could see how excited the lady sitting in front of me was. Nodding and smiling she replied, "Yes, that's him." However, I could also feel her heart sink – she missed him. Her deceased husband was talking to me really fast. I found myself trying to keep up with him. We were doing really well when suddenly he showed me a TV screen. I thought I was watching a horror film being played back to me, only it wasn't. I wasn't even sure I wanted to go where this lady's deceased husband was taking me.

I shifted around in my chair quite uncomfortably before I said, "Umm, this may sound a little crazy, but your husband is showing me a 'Wanted' sign above his head." Her face twisted as she replied, "Yes! He's talking about my son." I had a feeling this wasn't going to be good. I continued telling her, "Your husband is saying how your son's face is famous in America It's been on TV, but for all the wrong reasons." She nodded her head in dismay. I felt compelled to carry on as I told her, "He is also saying your son's been mentioned on the radio and featured in the newspapers, too. He's also on the run with a woman he says, darling." All the time the lady was nodding in agreement at her husband's reference to their son. It was clear how their son was a wanted man of interest to the police.

I could see tears filling the lady's eyes, so I looked at her and asked, "Are you OK to continue with this, or would you like to stop, darling?" She didn't hesitate in saying, "No! Please, you have to go on, I need to know." I continued with the reading and giving information until I found I could hardly swallow. I physically felt hands reaching for my throat. I felt as though I was choking through strangulation. This was not a good sign. Coughing, I told the lady, "I am so sorry, but your husband is putting his hands around my throat. Is this something your son did to you?" The lady, shaking her head and nodding said, "Yes, that's right. My son tried to strangle me. I'm afraid he wanted to kill me."

Sometimes, I wonder how much truth people want when they come to see me for a reading. So, I refrained from showing the lady the next few images her deceased husband was showing me. It seems their son had committed some heinous crimes. However, I did say to her, "Darling, your son will be caught with the woman he is fleeing with. He will also be serving a very long time in jail." She looked at me with hurt in her eyes as she said, "Yes, he will and so will she."

Whether the lady knew the extent of her son's crimes, I do not know.

All I know is how pleased she was with the reading. She thanked me for bringing in her husband and other family members. It made her happy they were watching over her, if only to protect her. I got up, walked around the table and gave the little lady a big hug. I prayed for God to protect her. I prayed her son and the woman he was running with would never ever be released from jail once caught. Anyone who takes the life of another should not be out on the streets.

Whilst I've known some people to be eager for readings, I had never known people to turn up over an hour early for a reading, which is exactly what happened at another Psychic Fayre I was working at. The doors hadn't opened to the public because the readers, including myself, had not set up our tables. Most of us had only just arrived when a short middle-aged Asian man walked in. He had a couple of other people in tow behind him. The organiser approached him and advised him to come back in just over an hour. He didn't leave.

I was busy setting up when I heard the man shout out, "All I want is proof of the afterlife, I just want to know if it's real." I didn't immediately recognise the man, but I did recognise his voice. I also remembered how he behaved the last time he was here, which was a bit erratic. He was the kind of person you would think would cause trouble. The loud type. But really, this man was just a big softie with a broken heart.

I shouted over to him, "Hello darling, didn't you see me last time?" Looking around he saw me move from behind my banner I was trying to position. He shouted, "Hello Carole. Yes, I did see you last time, but I want proof." I shouted back across to him, "I don't give proof darling, I give evidence. And didn't I give you that last time you were here - with your Dad, was it?"

Moving slowly towards me the man shouted, "Yes, you did Carole, and you were spot on with the stuff you gave me." He continued, "Even what happened after the reading you said would happen and did happen. You were spot on."

I concluded he didn't want more of, in his terms, 'proof.' What he wanted was for his Dad to connect to him again. I said, "Are you coming to me today for another reading then luv, or will you be going to someone else?" I was half hoping he would say the latter. He looked around the room at the other readers before he looked back at me. He replied, "No Carole, I'm coming to see you today, but I want proof my Dad is really in the afterlife." I looked at him and said, "Not a problem, you can come back when we open." He acknowledged he was early and apologised saying he would return when his sister arrived.

Since I had been so busy during the day I had not eaten. I popped downstairs to the restaurant and ordered a plate of chips and a pot of tea to take away. I do love a cup of tea. I needed to be fed and watered before the doors officially opened. It was going to be a nice night, I had a feeling. I took my little picnic back to my table. However, I hadn't finished dipping my chips in the tomato sauce when people started entering the hall. A lady walked towards me and asked, "Are you available." Removing my food from the table I placed it on the floor and nodded. I invited the lady to take a seat on the chair opposite me. The reading went really well; she was very happy.

With satisfied customers coming to me one after another, I was no closer to eating my very cold plate of chips. My tea had gone cold too. I continued to enjoy and embrace the love of Spirit Souls as they visited, one after another after another to connect their memories with loved ones. I didn't want to stop. The feeling of helping so many people was making me feel very proud. It was comforting.

Since I had no more people waiting for me, I thought I'd have a wander round the hall. I was just about to get up and have a stretch when the Asian man from earlier was rushing towards my table. His family was following on behind him. He looked really anxious as he said, "OK! Carole, can we have some more seats please and start?" All five of them had come together and wanted to sit together. I replied, "Sure, grab a few chairs from over by the door and bring them up." My table was a little over-crowded to say the least, but we were all comfy, which was the main thing.

When everyone was settled, I began the reading. Almost immediately I felt a Spirit energy stand close to me. He announced himself as 'Dad' and was the Father of most of this family present. He was once again going to give the evidence his family needed.

As this gentleman was connecting to me, he gave initials, a birth date and month. This turned out to be the initial and birthday of the young cousin sitting at the end of the table. They looked at me with a look of utter amazement and excitement. This family's Dad gave information related to birthdays and passing's connected to each of the young family that were sitting opposite and listening to me. There was not a dry eye coming from any of these people sat around my table. It was a very emotional moment for all of us, including me. I had to grab a tissue for myself.

This man, who had unceremoniously barged in before opening time, shouting out for proof, was now sitting quietly with a tissue in his hands covering his eyes and face. I looked at him and asked, "Are you OK, darling? Is that the evidence you needed to hear tonight?" His reply completely threw me as I was not prepared when he said, "Carole, it is Dad. I'm not crying because I don't believe you, I'm crying because I do believe you." I sat and watched him as he spoke with tears streaming down his face. He continued, "Carole, I'm crying because I want my Dad here with me. He should be here with us, not in the Spirit World." I could feel a lump form in my throat.

I was beside myself as I sat looking at this broken man sat in front of me. I knew and completely understood what he was saying. I knew what this man wanted, and I knew where he was coming from. I've been there myself many times, more times than I would have wanted to. I let him speak out and share his thoughts and feelings, which he had obviously been suppressing for some time. I gently and softly told him, "Darling, if Dad could come back in the physical form he would, but it's not a possibility and it's not going to happen." His tissue was mopping the tears running down his face as he nodded his head. I told him, "What is going to happen is that Dad, just as he is now, a beautiful spark of light in the Spirit World, has promised you right here today, he is never far away." I grabbed a tissue and wiped away my own tears.

His brother sitting with him broke in and said, "Listen to Carole, she's good at what she does. Dad is here, he wants you to believe and accept he isn't coming back." Thanking the brother for his words of comfort, I continued, "You now have to accept that you have been to me twice, and both times your Dad has given you indisputable evidence of his survival in the afterlife." Everyone was looking at me with tears in their eyes nodding in agreement. I looked at each person in this family and told them, "He can do nothing more than give you this evidence, so please accept it with his love and take it home with you."

After a few minutes I stood up, walked around to the other side of the table and took turns to hug and transfer the loving energies their Dad wanted me to give his family. I took turns to hug and hold each of his children and family that had come today to have a conversation with their Dad and Uncle. This is the love I was meant to give them today. I was happy to help them with this beautiful reunion. Yet, no matter how much evidence we can be given, sometimes even too much may still not be enough.

Chapter 20
Helping to Heal

I love my private readings with clients. So, when Karon, a friend of mine agreed to be filmed during a reading, it seemed like the door was open to everyone. We soon found out why.

I often meet up with Karon, who is really interested in my world. So, I wasn't surprised when she agreed to let me film her. I was grateful she was helping me with a new experiment and experience. I have been on TV a few times. I've had a good experience and a bad experience. I also had an invitation to appear as a psychic on a reality TV programme but turned it down. There were no editing rights I was allowed to control which concerned me. As I said before, people can sell your soul if they were going to make money from you.

Nonetheless, I wanted to expand my portfolio in my skill-sets. I wanted to perhaps build on filming for a mini web-series too. There's literally nothing productive when working with Spirit that I won't or can't do. I wanted to show people the reality of being a psychic medium.

I was lucky enough to borrow a nice little venue for the afternoon and Mark, a budding film entrepreneur volunteered to come along to direct and film too. Once filming began with Karon, we got off to a good start. Straight away a gentleman with a bicycle stepped in to visit. He would be on lead vocals for the reading. Meaning, he would be the one doing the talking and introducing other visiting Spirits.

As the conversation got started, I said to Karon, "OK, this gentleman wants to reference the month of January and April 13th as significant. Karon nodded her head in agreement saying, "Yes, I can take April 13th, it's my

Mother-in-Law's birthday." She couldn't take January at the time, but I knew it was important. The gentleman continued talking to us and I repeated his conversation to Karon telling her, "The 19th or 19 years is relevant, he says." Smiling Karon agreed and said, "Yes, that's my step-daughters age." I had to tell Karon her Mother in Law wanted talk about her side of the family. She wanted to let Karon know she was sending a lot of love and healing. There had been a loss in the family and this was her way of saying them up there were helping to heal all those involved. Karon was pleased to hear this. She confirmed there had been a sad loss.

The energy was continually changing around me, and I felt a lady to be visiting next. As she stepped forward, her conversation started straight away with her saying, "Tuesday was important, Carole. Tell Karon, I really did suffer before I passed, please." Adding, "You can tell her, too, I didn't like the hospital food, it was disgusting." I thought for one minute she was having a go at me, but when I mentioned to Karon how bossy her Mum was, she had to agree. And, Karon confirmed Tuesday was the day of her funeral. Karon's Mum didn't hold back as she went on, "February is significant." Turning to Karon, I asked, "Would you also understand why your Mum wants to reference February as being important, please?" There was no hesitation when Karon said with a smile on her face, "Yes, that's my Grandchild's birthday. It was important for that particular month to be referenced and identified because Karon's relationship with her ex was too. And, her Mum had plenty to say about that!

I thought we were finishing when another gentleman stepped forward. His energy was so calm and serene. Totally different to what I had just experienced with Karon's Mum, bless her. She was a very bossy lady. A bit like mine, in a way. Anyway, this man announced himself as Joseph. I said to Karon, "Would you understand Joseph, or Joe please, darling?" She answered, "Yes, he's my uncle, how lovely." After listening to Joe, I said to

Karon, "He wants to mention the museum, please." With a laugh Karon said, "I was talking about taking my little Grandson to the museum just this morning." There was so much more information that came out of Karon's visitors that I can't mention the whole reading here. But, once we were finished filming Karon was interviewed by Mark and confirmed many things to be true and correct. Things she had forgotten about. She was also feeling so much love around her too that it was nice for her. A love she once thought was impossible. I just want to say thank you to Karon and Mark for helping me with my little debut. And, I can honestly say, with hand on heart, even though Karon is a good friend, there was no information given to Karon that had been given before. I hardly ever give any client information from previous readings. This is something I tell Spirit not to do. If I have given repeat information, it is because the client needs to listen and take the information on board as being relevant.

Chapter 21
Show Time

Touching Heaven through my shows is a good night out for us all, in both worlds. I remember how a good night out used to be a nice beer or a *Spirit* in the local pub or club, but times have changed. People are now getting more interested in a different kind of Spirit. My kind of *Spirit*!

Sharing love, laughter and memories through the messages in my shows certainly does bring many people a sense of happiness and emotional healing. Having someone give evidence from over there and say 'Hello, I'm with you' is the best message a person could hope for. Sitting and sharing love and laughter between two worlds amongst a crowd takes the edge away from any nervousness felt during the show. People do get nervous because I'm going to be talking to 'dead' people who may be connected to them. Sometimes, too, a person can get nervous because I may openly reveal secrets they would rather not be aired. Much less in front of a crowd or a few hundred people.

Nerves are understandable. I've been there. I know how it can be scary. But I don't want anyone in my audience at my shows to be scared of anything. I want everyone to have a good old relaxing, positive, enlightening, empowering and lovable two-way, laid back, feet up, carefree experience with someone they love. Nothing less.

I know whenever I work. Spirit won't let me or my audience down. There will always be a *visitation and conversation* from someone in Heaven. I also believe working live can have its advantages, and its disadvantages. Either way, I embrace them both.

Anything can happen at my shows, and it usually does. For instance, I remember one show how it wasn't just my connection with Spirit that made a lady nervous, it was my false eye lash winking at her from the top of the microphone. When she was handed the microphone that was the first thing starring right back at her! I can't tell you how that in itself was a life-changing appearance for me, too. And, just for good measure, I whipped off the other lash and handed that one over to make a matching set. I was creased up laughing along with my audience. If ever there was a sight for 'spooky eyes' this would have been it. It was so funny. I said to the lady, "Itsy and Bitsy are a team, darling, you can't have one without the other!" Honestly, I have no idea how we all got through that message. It really was one hell of an 'eye-opener!'

People like my style of Mediumship because it's natural and down to earth. When I'm standing in front of an audience there is nothing fake or fancy about me as far as me or my messages go. What you see is what you get. Even if a set of false eye lashes named Itsy and Bitsy are involved.

I cannot question my sanity when I'm doing shows. Neither can I question how far I will go. That's something only Spirit knows. I Just know how I love doing shows. I love them because I know they are a place where I can get many messages across to many people in a short space of time. And I deliver quite a few. There's no shortage of deceased souls visiting to have a conversation when I open up my spirit door and Heaven's door. Basically, I'm like a kid with a new toy, I can't wait to get wound up and get started in reuniting family and friends. I love being in the company of a good few Spirits. All of whom want to talk.

There have been many times Spirit have introduced their own 'happy hour' into my shows, too. It happens when two or more Spirits step forward for a few different people at the same time. It's at that moment where there is a 'buy one get one free' message. It may be that there are similar names or similar commonalities between the souls who stepped forward. Yet, these souls are connecting to different people. All I know is at crazy times like these is how a cork is popped and a lot of 'Spirit' fills the room. Everyone is happy, if not confused. Even I get confused, and it's not too hard to confuse me, I may say. Put it this way, it's not uncommon for a couple of deceased loved ones to tag onto another deceased soul with the same similarities. Everyone is welcome and everyone who visits will be reunited with someone.

Every time I'm doing a show, I know how someone you love will make you laugh, and perhaps make you cry. Even me. But. either way, I can guarantee there will be plenty of watery eyes and wet faces. There will be no shortage of tissues being passed across everyone's head to reach the person who needs one. Even people not connected to the deceased souls will be crying and in need of a facial wipe.

Today, my stage work can include a dynamic of two platforms; I'm either giving an address in a Spiritualist Centre or I'm doing my own show. Of course, I'm no longer a DJ introducing the next number one hit single - I'm introducing people's deceased loved ones from the Spirit World. With this combination, I can reunite more souls closer to many more people. No matter how I do it, I just know I have to do it. The bigger the platform the bigger the voice.

Being out and about working with people and deceased loved ones at shows is my dream. It's my mission and my life. Over the years, I have found myself increasingly working for the Spirit World in a multitude of places. I have felt I am where I am supposed to be. I am putting myself amongst people giving messages to help them heal - not just from their loved ones in Heaven, but *with* their loved ones in Heaven.

Every platform I have ever stood on has been a stage for our lovely family, friends and loved ones in Heaven. Every platform has been and continues to be a place where messages can be received and given. Every stage is a platform for the voice of Spirit to be seen and heard. Every stage I've ever stood on has been for the purpose of reuniting families. The intended purpose is to reach out to both worlds and share a continuation of love between souls. It's important for those in heaven to be remembered and acknowledged, and it's important for us to acknowledge how they are the ones who have also had to adapt to change. They are the ones who are just as sad when they cross over because they have lost loved ones too. They are also the ones who need healing. Put yourself in their shoes, even if it's just for one moment.

The stage and the platform are a place to demonstrate and share a multitude of messages and memories to a wider audience. It's a place where love can be seen, heard, found and felt. If a stage or platform can be used to make the Spirit World and its residents famous, then I am proud to be a Medium who can stand on it and share their fame.

So, if anyone tells me I want fame from doing the work of a Medium, I'm going to tell them "Yes!" because I want people to know how I reunited someone's Mother, Father, Son, Daughter, Grandparent, Brother, Sister, Cousin, friend and any baby or sibling lost to the Spirit world. I'm going to tell people how I reunited someone's deceased loved one with their family and friends. I reunited them with an abundance of love, evidence and memories that cannot ever be broken. That is the fame I have been blessed with working as a Psychic and a Medium.

The Show Must Go On

'The Show Must Go On' was something I really did have to keep telling myself. I had a dream to work in a theatre with people's deceased loved ones standing next to me. I had a passion to reunite and bring people together from both worlds. I fulfilled this passion because I'm a firm believer if you want something, you have to go out and get it. I did exactly that.

Truthfully, I don't know how I did it, but I did. There were so many things that went wrong for me, I nearly ruined my biggest dream ever. It was my first time performing on a big stage within a theatre. I hadn't done a theatre venue like this with anyone before, let alone on my own. I remember thinking 'Fuck! What the hell have I done?' I wondered if I had been a little too ambitious in my dream. Nothing like throwing myself into the deep end. No harm in that, if you don't try you don't know as I always say.

I was happy as Larry when I had first booked a date to perform at the Howell Theatre, Brunel University, London. It felt like it was the right thing to do. It was something I didn't just want - but needed to do. Whatever happened, there would be no going back. It was me, myself, and I.

From my point of view, demonstrating at the University was the best place for me to be. It showed I had nothing to hide. I put posters up around the campus and advertised it well. I knew I was the real deal, so I wasn't worried. If I got slated, I got slated. But at the end of the day, you either believe in an afterlife or you don't. It is what it is. Nonetheless, the thought of what could happen to me after, and publicly, did cross my mind. But only the once. I would handle it no matter what. I'd handled worse in the past. I was one amongst millions of believers the world over.

I knew a few people at Brunel so arranging the theatre wasn't a problem. The only problem I had to overcome was the many health difficulties I was experiencing. Yet, I wasn't giving up. Giving up wasn't part of my plan. I spent months putting together advertising materials. It was too expensive to hire someone to do the artwork and design, so I took care of it all myself. My friend, Billy, thankfully, also gave a helping hand liaising and organising things. Things on that front were plain sailing.

When the night of the show finally came, I couldn't wait to start work. I felt like a curtain twitcher as I stood backstage peering from behind the curtains which filled the whole stage. Looking out, all I could see were rows and rows of seats filled with people. I was super excited. People were waiting for the visitations and conversations we would be participating in. It was exciting. It was also my biggest audience to date with almost three hundred people. It was Scary, I won't lie. But, excitingly scary.

I would have two audiences, one in front of me, the living, and one behind me, the living dead. Both would be patiently waiting to reunite to someone they love. It was a very special moment. Somehow, I didn't feel anything too negative would come out of this show. I felt certain the love from the audience and Heaven would be positive enough. In being honest, the only thing on my mind was helping those in Heaven connect to those who would be with us. Doing my job to my best ability was the only thing on my mind. Nothing more, nothing less.

Messages and memories can be shared anywhere in any place. My passion is always to help heal souls in both worlds. How can people slate that? Besides, it was the only theatre I could afford to hire. I tried to hire another local theatre, The Beck Theatre, Hayes, which I had set my heart on for many years, but they seemed to think I wasn't famous enough. They had a point, this was true. And, they the message I got was they had enough

Mediums hiring. However, even though they may not have heard of me, I had a good following they didn't know about. I knew I could have more than half filled their theatre. Never mind, I had a dream to fulfil and I needed a theatre. So, my alternative option was the one at Brunel University.

When obstacles are thrown in my way, I always tend to remove them where possible. My not being famous enough wasn't going to stop me living my dream. Disappointing as it was because I'd worked hard over the years to stand on that particular stage. However, my health could very well have prevented me from reaching any stage.

Yet, there it was, three weeks prior to the show I had an IBD (Irritable Bowel Disease) flare-up. Something I had suffered with for many years. Leading up to the show, I had been to three different hospitals for routine scans. I had cause to visit accident and emergency twice in acute pain. I also had reason to visit my doctor on four separate occasions. I thought I would have to cancel the show. I had to stop selling tickets just in case. My heart sank. I couldn't live with myself if I didn't do this.

All I could see, and feel was my big day and my dream, slowly drifting further and further away. It seemed like I wasn't going to recover from the extreme colitis flare-up. Yet, I wasn't going to be beaten. I told Hannah, my Spirit Guide, and them up there in Spirit that cancelling this show was not going to happen. I told them how I was doing this for them. The least they could do up there was make sure the show did go on – preferably with me in it.

Laying on a trolley in A&E one week prior to my show was a place I really didn't want to be. I was dehydrated and in a lot of pain. I was exasperated as I shouted at Spirit, "Don't you dare do this to me, don't you dare do this!" I was sobbing my heart out crying inside me tears of anger. I really didn't want to be in hospital. The wait alone was stressful enough.

When I was eventually seen, it was with a nurse who came into the cubicle. She was very chatty as she attempted to take my blood pressure. When she attached the nozzle to the tip of my finger, she looked at the reading on the machine. I could see she had a frown on her face as she looked at me asking, "Is your blood pressure normally this high, Carole?" I apologised and asked her to take it again. The second reading indicated my blood pressure was still too high. I smiled at the nurse and suggested she get another machine to take the reading. Of course, I forgot where I was because of the pain I was in. I was in hospital, there was a lot of dead people amongst me. I couldn't see them, but I could hear them. And, I felt their presence. It was not a good time for their visit, but I couldn't blame them. They wanted to talk to me. I didn't want to talk to them.

As the nurse left the cubicle, I had to tell the deceased souls to stand back. I was telling them I wasn't well. I told them how it was important for the nurse to obtain a true reading of my blood pressure. I told them on this occasion, they were 'getting in the way.' I reluctantly told them to 'go away'.

The nurse returned with a look of concern on her face and tried again. Third time lucky and the machine read right. My blood pressure was high, but not as high as the first machine had indicated on the previous two readings. The deceased souls had stood back. I was thankful, although I felt helpless, as I couldn't help those souls who had gathered round. I felt really guilty having had to send them away. It was for my best.

The date of the show was fast approaching. I was concerned and worried I wasn't going to be there. I didn't want to let people down. I didn't want to let Spirit down. I knew I couldn't possibly have any form of operation. I couldn't possibly have anything done that would keep me from standing on stage at my first theatre show. It was a moment I had worked so hard to achieve for a good number of years - I deserved to be there.

As I was laying on the trolley in a cubicle, I was still having conversations with Spirit and my Spirit Guides. I was shouting out to them in my mind, "You have given me almost a lifetime training and working for you. THIS is what I am meant to do, THIS cannot happen now!" My message to Spirit was loud and clear. I needed healing from them and I needed a lot. I put my health into their hands and asked for them to fix me. After an intravenous pain killer, an intravenous drip, an x-ray of my bowel and an overnight stay in hospital in A&E (Accident & Emergency), I could go home.

The problem had been due to the amount of pooh pooh I had in my bowel. Apparently, the nurse said I was full of 'shit!' Wouldn't be the first time I had heard that! But, I appreciated this version, at least it was the truth. Contrary to the 'normal' condition of colitis I usually suffered with, I found out I was constipated. All I needed to do was go home, take some medication, grab a good book and stay on the loo until everything came out rosy! That would be the pain relief I needed.

Because my mind and my focus had been detracted from the actual event, which was brought on through my illness, I wasn't prepared for the event, but I still wasn't going to cancel. I decided two days before the show I needed a stage set. I needed something that would feel Spiritual and homely for visitors from both worlds. I had to organise the set, my wardrobe, staffing and myself in the little time I had. This show was going to happen with me in it.

Because I couldn't afford anything flash or fancy for the stage, I had an idea in mind. I went out and bought over a dozen lanterns of all shapes and sizes. I bought some little battery-operated tea light candles to put around the theatre. I love lanterns and had a few scattered around my house which I would also make use of. I would also put LED angels and LED candles inside the lanterns to create a warm and glowing effect. I was overcome with emotion at what I had achieved in so little time. I had that proud feeling, something I very rarely have for myself.

I used two of my own large silver candelabras as props. These I placed at opposite ends of the stage standing on small tables. With these touches and props in place, I was ready. I wasn't well, but I was ready. I had a few good friends, including Karon, Billy, Beverley, Sonia, Karon, Lorraine, Dave and Sam who helped on the night. I was blessed. It was going to be OK. I wasn't going to cancel.

I knew how I would be taking a huge risk in demonstrating mediumship at a University. I knew how I would be risking my credibility and reputation. Only, it wouldn't be a risk at all. Because I believed in myself and believed in what I do. Demonstrating the afterlife was something I had been used to doing for many years. This wasn't going to be any different in terms of the job.

I would be in another world amongst academics and sceptics, yet, I wasn't afraid. I was confident and comfortable. I was genuine, I had nothing to hide. I was going to enjoy myself and the work ahead. We were all going to have a bloody good night out with one another and Heaven. I just had to tell myself to stop feeling so ill.

The day came for the show and I was feeling better than I had been, but not out of the woods by any means. My hair dresser Jord (who was with my Mum when she died) had done an exceptional job in colouring my hair. My other hairdresser, Sian, bless her, came back stage to tidy up my hair extensions before the show. She made me look good. They both did. I was looking as good as I was going to get. I just needed to have that 'feel good factor'.

I had also worked months to put together a screen presentation but hadn't quite finished it due to other work commitments, and my illness, of course. I had worked exceptionally hard to finish it off a day before the show. I was pleased with what I had produced. The end result was good. I had so much to do in so little time, but I did it. I pulled it off. But I knew I didn't do it alone, I knew Spirit was with me too every step of the way.

Spirit gave me the healing I needed. I am also a Reiki teacher (Japanese system of natural healing) so I was able to give myself a lot of Reiki energy to help with the pain. I began to feel better. No longer was I curtain twitching the long drapes backstage, I was out walking the boards of the stage to a round of applause. I was almost feeling like my old self once again. The moment was over-whelming. After what I had been through those last two weeks, the sound of people clapping was just what I needed to hear.

Nonetheless, truly, I couldn't believe I was there doing my own show in a theatre. I know it probably doesn't sound much, but to me, it was like winning the lottery. I could feel my eyes welling up with tears as I looked out at all the people in my audience who had come to see me. I looked out at everyone with pride in my heart knowing someone they loved would connect with a few of them. I was very emotional and could have cried just standing there. It was very surreal. I'm not one to show my emotions, especially when I know the people whom I am giving messages to are fighting their own.

I didn't feel nervous at all as I took hold of the microphone. It was something I had done many times before over the years. I had worked on many stages, albeit mostly a lot smaller. All I had to do was to keep telling myself how this stage was no different. I welcomed everyone with open arms. My door to Heaven and the Spirit World was open. Yay! Everyone in both worlds could take a seat. It was business as usual. I would help as many people and visitors from Heaven as I possibly could.

My dream of a wider audience and standing on stage in a real theatre had been accomplished. I had made a lot of people happy. We all did it together, both worlds. We made a lot of deceased souls, their family and friends very happy. I simply cannot, not, be a Medium - this is my life I love to share. I'm blessed, and we are all blessed in how we can continue to share in the love from our family and friends in the afterlife. There is no such thing as death. From what I know, everyone in Heaven is alive and kicking! Just ask them!

Tell Mum I Love Her

During my show at the Howell Theatre, Brunel University, my audience didn't have to wait long before a young man visited and opened the door to the Spirit World. I could feel his energy as he appeared on stage standing next to me. I turned to him as I acknowledged him and said, "Hello darling. Welcome. Who are you?" He didn't give a name but went straight into the memory he wanted me to connect to.

The gentleman standing next to me was tall and had facial stubble. He wore scruffy jeans with a well-worn t-shirt hidden well beneath his black leather jacket. I saw his motor bike was by his side, his body slumped next to it. I was ready to work and had enough information to give out.

Looking out into my audience with my microphone in my hand, I gave the description of the man standing next to me. I described him just as he was showing himself to me. I called out to my audience how this lovely man's bike was important to him. I asked him for more information and he told me, "I was found by the bridge." I felt a sense of serenity and calmness as he spoke to me. He continued telling me, "Carole, I was involved in drugs, they took my life. Tell my Mum, tell her I'm sorry."

For the life of me I don't know how I managed to keep on my feet. I wanted to sit down, I wanted to hug this young man. I wanted to apologise to this young man for those who were involved in taking his life by supplying him with the drugs he had taken.

I looked around the theatre to see who would connect to this desperate young man. As I repeated what he had said I could hear a few voices chattering. I looked deep into the audience to see a hand being raised. I could hear a voice, but I couldn't see the face of the lady the voice was connected to. The spot lights were shining in my face and it was difficult to see out into my audience. I don't like bright lights, so I didn't have all the house lights turned up. I worked on voice vibration from where the lady was sitting.

I asked the lady who had raised her hand if she could take everything I had given on behalf of the deceased soul. She confirmed she could, and confirmed he was her brother. I said, "He's saying, "Tell Mum I love her." I felt a lump in the back of my throat as he said this. His sister accepted all the information her brother had given. She replied, "I know what he means, thank you."

It felt good knowing I had helped this man and beautiful soul in Heaven connect to his sister. His sister, who could pass his loving message onto his Mum, their Mum. I was sorry for this lady's loss. I was sorry for her family's loss. I was sorry for the loss of the young man, her brother, as he didn't deserve to die the way he had. His presence with the evidence he gave was applauded and appreciated. His Mum would have been proud of her son bringing through a message of not just love, but his survival in the afterlife. That thought alone would be very comforting to her.

Just Popping Out

I was demonstrating at a show with a full house at a golf club when a deceased gentleman took the opportunity to visit. He stepped in next to me. I turned to him and said, "Hello darling, what can you tell me?" He replied, "I'm Nigel." I saw how he was wearing a clean white shirt with sharp pressed trousers. He looked very smart. I could hear and physically feel he had a breathing problem.

In listening to the man standing next to me, I was ready to make his connection and have a conversation with someone in my audience. Taking hold of the microphone I was calling out, "I have a gentleman with me who has announced himself as 'Nigel.' I paused for a moment to get my breath before saying, "He has also indicated a breathing problem, can anyone take this gentleman, please?" I could see a few shakes of the head in the crowded hall. No takers, so I continued, "This lovely man is very well spoken, posh-like, and he wants to connect to the date 11th October." There were also two other dates I connected to, as well, and gave them out. I was asking, "I'm looking for someone who can take 'Nigel', a breathing problem, smart dresser, October 11th?" Again, no takers. No raised hands, just people looking at me looking at everyone else in the hall and waiting for someone's hand to go up.

I turned to Nigel and asked, "Is there anything else you can give me darling?" He did not hesitate as he said the names 'Maggie' and 'Graham.' Smiling out at my audience I said, "Please, this gentleman wants to connect to 'Maggie' and 'Graham', too." I then added, "Is anybody there for this lovely man?"

I looked at Nigel and said, "Thank you darling, you're doing really well." I was looking out into the audience for a raised hand. It was a moment of madness when a lady, whose name we got to know as Sonia, was standing at the back of the hall raised her hand. The hall was packed, people were almost sitting on one another's laps. Even though I loved this club, I realised how I needed to book into a bigger venue. There were far too many people for its size.

Looking at the lady across the packed hall, I spoke into the mic and said, "Hello lovely, what can you take please?" Her reply came back, "I can take all that information. That's my Granddad, Nigel." Everyone turned around to see a young lady standing at the back shouting back down to me. She was eager to carry on as she replied back, "I can take 11th October which is my Mum's birthday, the two other dates are his son's birthdays." She went on to confirm, "Maggie and Graham are his children."

Sonia's Granddad had a message specifically for her, as well. As I spoke on his behalf, I told Sonia, "He said to tell you he was with you in hospital, darling. He knows how you needed a lot of love and a lot of healing." Sonia confirmed this to be true. I said, "He wants you to know your sister is going through a difficult time and he knows about it." Sonia confirmed all this to be true, too. Then, her Granddad told her, "Your sister will get married."

I gave Sonia a wedding date to give to her sister – she confirmed this date to be very important. The date was the same as their Granddad's own wedding anniversary. It was a heart-felt, very much needed message. I was overjoyed at the evidence Nigel gave that I was able to give to his Granddaughter. I could see people's faces looking shocked as I was delivering all this evidential and accurate information. To me, 'The Messengers' always surprise me, yet, never surprise me!

The most amazing thing about this message is how Sonia only popped into the venue to pick someone up on the way home from a hospital appointment. Well, she wasn't the only one who had big ideas about popping in. It was quite clear her loved ones over there wanted to pop-in, too. To say Sonia was in shock was an understatement. She couldn't believe what had just happened to her. And, I know how that one experience changed her life forever.

Even today, I am reminded by Sonia, who has also become a lovely friend, of how she wasn't meant to be there. I'm glad she did pop-in because I love the friendship Sonia and I now have. Thanks to her Granddad. Who knows who's going to 'pop-in' where or when!

I Only Came for a Laugh

I do love a bit of a giggle, but don't we all? We all do those silly things that make us laugh. We all go to places that we normally wouldn't that are out of our comfort zone. We meet people we normally wouldn't meet. We can never be prepared who we will meet no matter where we go, so a surprise is always nice. Surprises can happen all the time at my shows – Spirit never fail to surprise someone. Truthfully, I never know who is going to surprise me either: the 'living', the 'dead' or both!

Me and my audiences, we click. We have a good time. Enjoying ourselves is always something we most certainly like to do. However, I do recall a very sceptic lady at a show I was demonstrating at. I remember her because she was definitely surprised as members of her spirit family came to visit. She was so surprised it rendered her speechless. I, too, recall how incredibly amazing the energy felt as it was being shared by everyone in both worlds at the show.

I say with hand on heart I have loved and appreciated every single person who has ever sat in my audience – from believers to disbelievers. The only ones that I shut down are the noisy ones, the ones who relentlessly chatter all the way through someone else's message.

Anyway, back to the show and the lady who was 'sceptic.' We were all having a really good time as there were lots of Spirit present. And, I could feel the presence of one special visitor in a spirit lady step forward. I acknowledged and welcomed her, as I always do as a matter of courtesy. We always say 'hello' to people we meet, Spirit are no different.

The deceased lady whom had stepped forward did so with an air of importance. There was someone here she wanted to connect to. I acknowledged her and said, "Hello darling, how can I help you please?" She spoke telling me, "I'm Sheila." I was happy at how she came straight in and wasted no time in communicating. We were off to a good start. With the information she gave, I called out, "I have a lovely lady who has stepped forward to join us. Her name is Sheila and recently passed. She wants to acknowledge June, December and these dates (omitted) as important. Can anyone take this lovely lady please?"

I found myself repeating the given information as I looked out into my audience. There were many smiling faces looking back at me. This lady's energy made me go all goose-bumpy. That happens during a visitation from an over-excited deceased soul. With the hall filled to capacity, I could feel how everyone would want to get a message from someone in Heaven. Sadly, I knew only too well that not everyone would. Many people come to feel the love Heaven brings and would be OK if today wasn't for them. Many people just come to feel loved and know they can get that even without a message.

I found myself pacing the floor side to side. I was looking out into my audience waiting for a hand to go up. It didn't happen. Turning to the lovely Spirit lady, I asked her, "Can you give me a little more please darling?" She responded by saying, "Yes! Mike's here, too." I thanked her and told her she would be OK, we would get her connection. Turning back to my audience I was calling out impulsively through the microphone all the information I had been given. I got nothing. No one spoke, no one raised their hand, my words were met with silence. I was looking out into my audience, who were looking back at me. They were still smiling – always a good sign.

I've been a Medium for too long to panic or get flustered. I was right with the information and I knew the deceased lady I was helping was right.

Spirit never lets me down. The connection was here. I was determined I was going to find it. I needed to reunite this beautiful lady with someone here in my audience. I needed to share memories in this message with her person here. Her person had to be here. I wasn't giving up on her, that's not my style. A reunion needed to take place. I kept going, giving information relating to dates and months of significance. Still, no one raised their hand. I couldn't ignore the evidence I was being given. I needed to work with it and work with the lovely Spirit lady.

I repeated the names and dates out loud for good measure. I had to keep going until the person who I needed to reunite with raised their hand. I would keep going until someone gave me a nod or a sign. I needed someone to tell me this connection was with them.

People were looking back at me with blank faces, a few shrugging their shoulders. People don't always raise their hand. People can be surprised and shocked when someone they know steps forward to visit and it's for them. Not everyone will expect to get something. What I do know is how no one can come to my show and not expect to be part of it. Everyone has a part in my show, and everyone is not only part of my show, but they are part of the 'Spirit World', too – even if only for a few hours.

People have many reasons not to take someone from Heaven. The most popular reason is because they didn't like them, or even hated them. Sometimes there are those who will be too embarrassed to raise their hand and won't. Then there are the ones who have secrets that don't want their dead to share with everyone else, much less to hundreds of people. It happens. Also, don't come to see me if you're planning a surprise for someone, including if you're having an affair with your best friend's Hubby! I can't promise those over there or me as the messenger will keep your secret safe. Funnily enough, secrets have a haunting way of coming back, especially from the grave. I'm not joking!

Anyway, what seemed like a good ten minutes was really only a matter of seconds. It's not always the dead I have to raise, but the living, too! I always call out loud and clear on behalf of the deceased soul first. I do this work for them, so I have to do my best. So, it looked like no one was going to take the lady, or the information she was giving me. I wasn't getting anywhere and knew I had to move on. However, not before I gave it another try. I looked out at my audience asking, "Last chance, either phone a friend, ask the audience or go 50/50. Who can take this lady, please?"

You could hear a pin drop as everyone looked around to see who would raise their hand. Like me, people wanted someone to raise their hand. My search had finally ceased as my eyes met with a lady sitting in the middle row. It was love at first sight. She raised her hand and burst out crying, she knew I was coming to her. This was the lady I needed to reunite with.

The lady confirmed her name was Sheila. She acknowledged June was her deceased sister standing next to me. I felt relieved and happy for June in that her sister had finally connected with her. We had enough information with the names, dates, months and years along with other evidence between us to carry on. So, we did, and what a wonderful message it turned out to be.

Besides all the information and evidence that was already given, here's how a bit more of it went … June (Spirit side) was telling Sheila to 'get out more.' Sheila nodded her head in disbelief and laughed. Then I felt another Spirit soul slide in and stand next to me. He announced himself as Mike, whom June had introduced him earlier. Anyway, Sheila accepted him as her husband. He referenced dates significant to his passing, plus dates of relevant birthdays. All was true and accepted by Sheila. All good evidence. Unfortunately, before I could say anything else, I felt Mike's energy draw back. He was leaving.

Now, I really was disappointed as I had to tell Sheila, "I'm sorry darling … he's gone!" I looked at her telling her, "He didn't seem keen to say anything else, luvvie." The room filled with laughter as Sheila shouted out, "I wouldn't want him to!" Placing a hand over her mouth and shaking, Sheila was in hysterics. You could have knocked me over with a feather as she said, "*I only came for a laugh* because my son told me to come. It was his idea, he wanted me to get out more, as well!" That did it, everyone was laughing, myself included.

I was so pleased Sheila had come along, and it was obvious she was meant to. We were all pleased for her. Whether it was for a laugh, or not, her sister and husband gave her, and us a moment of love, laughter and tears of happiness. Everyone was happy.

At most of my shows, sadly, there will always be that one person who will put their hand up in desperation to take anyone, but they shouldn't. It's not fair. As hard as it is, giving away, or connecting a deceased loved one to the wrong person is something I can't allow. If I did, then the deceased loved one could end up with Mr. or Mrs. Wrong, who is nothing to do with the deceased Soul. I'm not a Medium who will make things 'FIT' for the sake of grace and saving my face. Fortunately, Sheila was Mrs. Right.

After the show, Sheila came up to me and thanked me for her message. I gave her a hug as I chatted with her. She told me how she couldn't believe her recently deceased sister, June, had come through to reunite with her. She mentioned she was a sceptic, didn't believe in the Spirit World, or a life after death. She didn't want to accept the visit from her sister because she didn't believe.

Sheila herself was in her 80s. Yet, those ten minutes I had connected with her, had made her happy, changed her life, and she was no longer a sceptic. I make people happy, I'm a 'Medium' and this is what I do. I connect and reunite loved ones with memories, love, emotions and evidence of survival on the Other Side. I give back to people part of their loved one's journey after they transition to Heaven. Even if it's only for a few moments.

Grandads Poppy

Talking about my LIVE shows and some of the messages I have delivered is something I love to do. And because the messages are delivered to a public audience, I want to share them here, too. Because there really are some beautiful messages that really move not just me or the person(s) receiving the message, they also moved the whole audience as well. And, this next message … almost didn't happen. Yet, it was a message that turned out to be extremely heart-felt, meaningful and memorable.

It was the second half of a show that was about to commence. There had been a family arriving late who managed to grab a few chairs and sit at the back. I was welcoming everyone back once again when I was joined by a deceased elderly gentleman. He was pulling on my elbow as he impatiently stood by my side. He was dead eager for me to get a move on and talk to him. He wanted to get the conversation started so he could have a good old natter with his loved ones.

As I turned to acknowledge him, I said, "Hello darling, what's your name please?" He looked at me with a nervous smile as he replied, "I'm Frank." I didn't want him to be afraid, so, without sounding like I was chatting him up, I told him "You have a nice smile, darling." It was the type of smile that melted your heart. I know only too well how deceased souls get nervous when they visit, so I converse with all of them as a friend, which I am, technically. I wanted to make Frank feel comfortable. Believe it or not, it can be nerve-wrecking for Spirit too.

Frank spoke softly as he gave October 3rd as significant and important. I was ready to make the reunion happen. I just knew he would be for someone here in my audience as I spoke through the microphone saying, "I have a lovely elderly gentleman here, his name is 'Frank' and he references October 3rd as important." I continued, "He also makes me feel a little breathless, too, bless him." I could see a few raised hands from the family that arrived late sat at the back of the hall. They accepted Frank as their Father and Grandfather, respectively. There were quite a few of them and I was really pleased they had made it, as their conversation would prove.

Frank was connecting to one of his daughters as he gave a lot of evidence throughout the message. His family members were all very pleased, if not shocked, at the evidence Frank was giving. Frank knew it, too, as he referenced the memory in how his Grandson had smashed a window. He had done it whilst replacing the old one. As I mentioned this, Frank teasingly said to his Grandson, "That didn't go very well, did it?" I think my screwed-up face said it all as the family and everyone in the hall burst out laughing, as you do! For some reason, we always seem to enjoy laughing at other people's misdemeanours. Yes, we do! haven't you?

Anyway, I thought the conversation was over when I saw Frank turn to leave and head towards my Spirit door. Instead of leaving though he turned back to me. He placed a poppy in my hand. I acknowledged it as a parting gift from him to his family. I knew it was going to be important, so I looked straight at his daughter and asked, "Darling, would you understand why Frank wants to give you a poppy, please?" I could see the family all smile at the same time as his daughter confirmed this was very significant. She replied, "Yes, Dad ordered a poppy off the internet in remembrance of his own Dad." I smiled as she continued saying, "Unfortunately, Dad died before the poppy arrived, so he didn't get to see it." I could see how Frank was shaking his head in disagreement. I responded, "No, darling, that's not right, he did see it. He said he wants you to remember his poppy with pride." A beautiful reunion and conversation took place with a memory of a gift that was nearly missed - had the family not made it in time for the second half.

Happy Halloween

Usually around Halloween I try to organise something in my diary. It will either be a show or a psychic supper. It's a good opportunity for people to dress up, an opportunity to look weird, spooky and ghostly in Halloween costumes. Well, it would be rude not to organise something special on this important, very commercial night of the year ... wouldn't it? After all, Halloween is thought to be associated with the Celtic festival 'Samhain' when ghosts and Spirits are celebrated.

The last Halloween event I organised was a psychic supper. I'd been invited to host the event in a beautiful venue by a small pond. It was certainly a night to remember. In fact, one I doubt anyone could forget. I know I won't, but happy to say for good reason.

People had turned up in some amazing costumes, from the 'Grim Reaper' to 'Batman' to ghostly figures, skeletons and witches. Naturally, after everyone had eaten their supper, it was time to serve another kind of supper, from the real 'Spirits.' My demonstrations in connecting, communicating and linking Spirit souls to their loved ones was going really well, at least, right up until an elderly gentleman stepped forward to join the party. Once this man started to talk he didn't want to stop. Nor did he want to leave. And it wasn't like I could push him out the door, either, because you can't push Spirit anywhere. Yet, this gentleman wanted to hog the floor and demonstrate how he could talk for England, literally!

The moment I felt his energy as he stepped forward, I turned to acknowledge him and said, "Hello darling, who are you?" He said, "Bill, I'm Bill." Thanking him for joining us, I asked him for more information. He made sure I would have plenty to keep us all going, if not for most of the night!

Looking out at all the painted faces and the people behind the masks, I spoke into my microphone saying, "I have a lovely gentleman here by the name of Bill." As I could see what Bill looked like I started to describe him to my audience. Bill was making my chest and lungs ache. This can be my sign for a heart, lung, emphysema, chest, or a cancerous condition. But, I knew what he had as he told me. When I'm not directly told of the chest condition, I can feel an energy on my chest. Even so, I could give this condition, so, I said, "I feel this gentleman would have lost a subsequent amount of weight. I continued, "I also feel perhaps he would have passed with a cancerous chest and lung condition, bless him."

Reaching out to a small group of lovely ladies sat in front of me, I asked, "Darlings ... can anyone here take this lovely gentleman, Bill, who had a cancer condition, please?" Straight away a lady raised her hand and shouted back at me with a lot of excitement and enthusiasm, "I can!" The connection was made. A reunion had commenced.

Bill gave me two names, 'Frank' and 'John.' For the benefit of the audience, I said to the lady who was holding the microphone that had been handed to her, "Hello darling, thank you. How do you connect to the names Frank and John, please?" She instantly replied, "They are the names of Bill's two sons." I could see Bill smiling as he was standing next to me. He looked proud to see someone from his family here had recognised him. He was happy to be reunited. He wanted to chat and took the opportunity. For the life of me I can't tell you how Bill made the most of this opportunity. But he did!

Bill kept chatting away giving me more and more information. I couldn't keep up with him. Whatever he was on I wanted some of it! He was an excellent communicator. He knew what to do and was doing it well. All the time he was talking to me, I had to remember what he was saying. He was really talking fast. Unfortunately for me, my ability to retain information is like pouring flour into a sieve, it doesn't stay there very long. Whatever I get has to be given at the same time Spirit gives it.

The lady confirmed Bill to be her Granddad. She was really pleased he had come to the party. I asked her, "Would you understand the year 1952, three children, a bad back, the numbers 22 and 27 and April being significant, please?" She didn't hesitate in her reply as she said, "Yes, I can take all of that, I have three children, and I also have a bad back". I was just about to ask about the dates when she continued, "The dates are birthdays with one belonging to my Mum, his daughter, of course, and 1952 was the year she was born." Taking a deep breath, the lady added, "Oh! April is my birthday, too." Everyone was happy and in awe of the evidence in this message. Not only were Spirit flowing well, but the love was, too, in every message.

I could see how Bill had made his Granddaughter really happy, and her friends who were sat at her table were smiling and perhaps a little bit shocked. It's always nice to be happy for others receiving messages, quite often they are the ones who need them more. We were all happy for her, including Bill. I thanked the lady for connecting with her Granddad. It was a very lovely and very special moment.

I was ready for my next link as I held the microphone and said, "OK, I'm hearing the name, Sam." Before I could continue, I could see the lady who I had just disconnected with put her hand over her face. Now this was spooky! She looked at me in total disbelief. But, she laughed and said, "Yes, my name is Sam!" I laughed as I said, "Oh, bloody hell! Your Granddad hasn't finished talking to you darling, I'm not sure he wants to, either!" A round of laughter and applause followed. I thanked Sam once again for linking in with me and her Granddad.

OK, this was ... interesting. I turned to Bill and thanked him once again. I mentioned to him under my breath, as you do, how he should step back into the light so other deceased souls could visit. Sometimes Spirit really think they can push it by overstaying their welcome. Like people, there are those who are the 'life' and 'soul' of the party. Bill was ours. And, who would blame them?

Nonetheless, when there are quite a few people in my audience, I always try to give out as many messages as I can, from different loved ones. After all, it's only fair. However, what Spirit want and what I want can sometimes be two different things … As Bill proved.

Since we had all been laughing so much at Bill and his persistence, I didn't know who was talking to me when I heard the link to the next message. Anyway, I had the link, so I called out, "Does anyone have a problem with a television, please, because I am hearing a problem with a TV?" The room went eerily quiet. No one answered, and no one raised their hand. Suddenly, Sam shouted to me, "My Granddad was a TV engineer!" I looked at her and burst out laughing as I told her, "Granddad, he's not going to leave is he, bless? Happy Halloween!" Everyone was laughing. It seemed Bill just didn't want to go. He was having a good time. He just kept talking … and talking. He was giving evidence. He had his moment, and he made the most of it. Well, wouldn't you?

My Old Mans a Dustman

I often wonder where Spirit dig old songs up from when I'm working. Yet, it's not for me to choose their song choice, it's theirs. However, I do know the songs they ask me to reference are always meaningful, or significant. Just as they are significant to the person receiving the memory of that song. Almost everyone has a favourite song that reminds them of something or someone. Including right down to a specific time of their life.

Songs often come up at shows, which I'm glad they do, mostly. I just don't like having to sing them. Nonetheless. sometimes I have to in order to jog someone's memory. Even so, I'm sure the Spirit, the person and my audience all despair when I attempt to sing. I can't sing for toffees. Even I would have to agree. Which brings me to recall a demonstration at a show I was at where my display of screeching vocals didn't do me, or anyone else justice. A deceased soul stepping forward wanted me to sing. Perhaps he couldn't sing either - but he announced himself as 'Ray.' He had a lot of energy to use and was going to use it.

After I announced his name to my audience and the condition he passed with, Ray was acknowledged and accepted by two lovely ladies. He couldn't wait to get going and start the reunion with his memories. And, he didn't stop talking as he gave some significant evidence along with a few dates, all of which were also accepted. But, the best piece of evidence was yet to come.

As I've said, I'm not a 'singer' by any means. I've dabbled with music as a DJ, and I've sung along to songs with Spirit in private. There have been many times in many places too where I have awkwardly sung out of tune on behalf of Spirit. But, songs are very good evidence, so I have to give them.

Anyway, Ray had me tapping my foot and singing along to Lonnie Donnigan's 1960s classic, "My Old Man's a Dustman, he wears a dustman's hat, he wears cor blimey trousers, and he lives in a council flat, Oi!" I remembered it quite well, fortunately. Even though I couldn't sing, I was feeling really happy as Ray and I sang along to the words. Based on my vocals, I'd never win a talent contest that's for sure. However, it wasn't my happiness I was sharing. It was the happiness of the deceased soul, Ray. I was doing this for him.

After my brief and hilarious rendition of Donnigans' classic, I looked at the ladies laughing as I asked, with tongue in cheek, "Does My Old Man's a Dustman song mean anything to you, please?" They looked at each other laughing, as was everyone else. Mostly at my crap singing I had had the misfortune of demonstrating. The ladies looked at me puzzled shaking their heads saying, "No, sorry Carole, we can't place that one." I laughed, we all laughed as I told them, "Hold onto that song, it's going to mean something."

I thanked the ladies for the connection and left Ray's love and memories with them. I don't mind telling you, I kept singing that bloody song in my head right through until the next day, and beyond. It was simply annoying … In an amusing sort of way.

I was chuffed when I received a lovely message from one of the ladies the very next day. She confirmed how she had spoken to her Dad about the message from Ray. She had mentioned the song, 'My Old Man's a Dust-man' too. And, to her surprise, her Dad told her Ray had given him some CD's the day before he passed to the Spirit World. On both of them checking through the stack of CD's they really did find Lonnie Donnigan, 'My Old Man's a Dustman.' Perhaps it was Ray's way of telling his friend to play his favourite song now and then.

Good News! Bad News! My News!

Mum is always looking after me from her world in Heaven. Even when I went into hospital for an operation, Mum was there with me. It had been a bad time for me to get ill with so many shows to cover. I had a lot of work coming in that needed me in good health with positive energy. I needed to get through it all. However, I was glad my health concerns were now being investigated.

I was really looking forward to my operation. I'd had lots of intrusive scans over the months and plenty of blood tests. I was looking forward to knowing that the root of my problem was now being removed. There's nothing worse than being in pain when you have to work. Going into hospital was my opportunity to get rid of the pain once and for all. My Gynaecologist had discovered an unidentified lump on my ovary and another in my womb. I felt at last it could all hopefully be resolved. Or, at least so I thought. But, no, it wasn't resolved because it wasn't that simple.

I arrived at the hospital and checked into the ward. I was surprised to be greeted by a lovely nurse who called my name and welcomed me. There was something in the way she was connecting to me that made me feel I should know her. After a few minutes it clicked, I did know her. She was one of my clients. I was pleased I would be in such good hands.

I swapped my day wear for their sexy (you've worn them, too?!) see through 'ward' wear and made myself comfy on the trolley. This was going to be my bed for as long as I needed it. I told Hubby he didn't need to wait and sent him home. Much to his reluctance. I didn't see the point of him sitting waiting for me for God knows how long. Besides, I wasn't nervous.

I knew I was in good hands. I was fortunate to be under the care of the Gynaecologist who did our IVF (In Vitro Fertility) treatment over twenty plus years ago. It failed. Sadly, it happens. Nonetheless, I trusted him implicitly to do what was needed with the operation I was now going to have.

I had taken a book to read in case I was there for the day or longer. I needed to distract myself from all the deceased souls who would visit me. There would be many of them, of this I was sure. There are a lot of deceased souls in hospitals and I couldn't afford any distractions. I had asked my guides for some privacy from Spirit. I couldn't be connecting and communicating to any dead Spirits on this occasion. I needed to be normal 'Carole' not 'Carole the Medium.' The only Spirits I asked to be present were my healing guides. I asked them to be present during the operation and asked them to help if help was needed.

There was a lot of hustle and bustle with the nurses and patients going on around me, so I picked up my book. I didn't want to hear of any symptoms anyone was experiencing. Neither did I want to hear of the types of operations patients were going to have. I didn't want to pick up on their energy that would affect my own. Being a Physical Medium I couldn't afford to take on someone else's pain or condition.

I had taken a book along by Theresa Caputo, *The Long Island Medium*, and started to read it when another familiar face came over to see me, a friend of mine and theatre nurse, Kay. She had heard I was on the ward and kindly popped along to visit me. I hadn't seen her for a while so was pleased to reconnect. We chatted for a few minutes before she went on her way. Seemed there were many nurses who were my clients working on the ward. Still, it was good to know how I was amongst a few good friends and in good company. Tea would be on tap.

With all the distractions from the nurses and doctors coming and going to their patients, I put my book down. I couldn't concentrate. My thoughts turned to my operation. I was waiting for the call and my turn to go down to theatre. I was wondering what the Doctor's would find once the camera was inserted into my abdomen. I was wondering what news I could expect to hear. Sometimes, when it's about me, I don't always pick up on things, so I generally just leave it to the experts. It's not in my control, anyway. What will be will be, whatever the outcome I would deal with it.

However, the longer I waited the more I couldn't help thinking about what the Doctor's *would* be telling me after the operation. I was trying to use my psychic sense as I wondered if it would be good news or bad news. I wasn't scared. In fact, I felt calm and relaxed considering. I was having my ovaries out, it was a big deal. As I was thinking about the Doctor's verdict and what he might say, I heard a voice speaking to me. I heard a voice say, "Don't worry Carole, it's good news and bad news, but it's nothing to worry about."

I looked across to where the voice was coming from and saw Mum sitting in the chair next to me. Tears filled my eyes. Mums eyes welled up, too, as she always did whenever I was in hospital. Mums do that, don't they? Shed a tear for their unwell child no matter how old they are. Even at my young age of fifty-something, Mum was still worried about me.

Having Mum there with me was a pleasant surprise. I never expected her, nor did it cross my mind that she may be there. However, she didn't stay, she didn't need to. She let me know how she was still looking after me, even from Heaven. And she reassured me as she told me, "You have nothing to worry about." I found her words comforting. Before she went, she said, "Carole, you'll be alright." I believed her.

One of the doctors who performed my operation came to visit me after and told me, "I've got good news and bad news Carole." Déjà vu! I looked at her and said, "I knew you were going to say that." Mum was right, there was good news, I had nothing nasty like cancer. The bad news, I still had my ovaries!

I remember thinking it wasn't good. It wasn't what I wanted to hear. Yet, it was better than I had expected. I really didn't know whether to laugh or cry. I had gone to have my ovaries removed but sods bloody law they came back with me. Talk about feeling cheated! I really wanted those buggers out to prevent any nasties later on. But because of previous operations to drain fallopian cysts, there were too many adhesions sticking my ovaries to my bowel making the procedure impossible. Nothing in my life is ever simple.

Despite the news, I couldn't complain on this occasion. And, I don't often get to see Mum in physical form, unless she feels it necessary. I was pleased how this was one of those necessary times.

Fanny

It was quite an amusing experience for a widow when her two deceased husbands made an appearance at one of my shows. It was also a full house. Anything could happen, and it did! It wasn't just me who brought 'Spirit' along, because most of the crowd did too. It was going to be a good night, I could tell from the giggles and energy in the hall. People wouldn't just be consumed with 'Spirit' - they would be embraced by 'Spirit' too.

Anyway, as I was working, I was paying attention to a deceased gentleman. He had stepped forward ready to connect and communicate in more ways than one. I could see all I needed to see to describe him. I could see how he was wearing denims with turn ups. He also had a little body odour that drifted over me. He gave his own name, his Granddaughters name and dates that would be significant. I could see he was having problems breathing which was an indication of the way he passed.

As I gave information to my audience about the way the gentleman passed, to the clothes he was wearing, a young lady raised her hand. I made sure she could connect to the names and dates I had given before I continued. I could see from her face she was a little shocked, but she also had a nervous giggle about her too. I acknowledged her as I asked her, "Hello darling, which part of the information can you take please?" She replied, "All of it. I can take all of it. It's my ex-husband!"

I was getting more dates and a different kind of passing when I felt the energy changing. Another visitor had stepped forward of a deceased gentleman. I described him and the way he passed and asked, "Can you take this gentleman too please lovely?" The lady was really excited as she replied, "Yes! they are both my ex-husbands." The audience roared with laughter, as did I when I asked, "Is this a good thing or not darling?" More laughter came. Well, two exes' just like that - no one could have expected that. I was glad she could see the funny side. As could we all.

However, the laughter didn't stop there. One of her beloveds wanted me to reference 'Fanny.' Well, he had been her ex-husband after all. I had to ask him more than once if this was the name he wanted me to give. I felt he was pulling my leg, having a laugh with me. I had a feeling his humour was going to get me into trouble. He assured me it was a reference he wanted me to make. I obliged as I asked the lady, "Umm, can you connect to the name 'Fanny', or know why one of your husband's want to acknowledge a 'Fanny?" By now the whole hall was in tears of laughter. Like me, they seemed to know where this was going too. I couldn't keep a straight face if I tried, and believe me, I did try. I also didn't know how I got through that message, but I did. And, unsurprisingly, I knew what was coming next. After I managed to compose myself the best way I could, I asked the lady, "He wants me to ask if you've been 'putting it about a bit' darling - the fanny?" Well ... there wasn't a dry eye amongst us.

Thankfully, through her tears, my tears, and everyone else's tears of laughter his widowed wife confirmed it was his way of having a joke on her. She confirmed how this is something he would definitely do to embarrass her, and something he would definitely say. Bless. Personally, that message was one of the most amusing messages I think I have ever had to deliver. Well done to both ex-husbands, the widow and the audience for bringing such entertainment value along. The love along with the evidence was undeniable. It all meant so much to the one person who was so special to those who were so important.

Naughty Nurse

Spirit really do have a good sense of humour and love to show off to us. I remember this from one show when a deceased male stepped forward to visit. He indicated how he wanted to speak to the 'Nurse.' As he was talking to me, he showed me an image of a young lady dressed up in a nurse's uniform. I remember thinking how this message was going to go one of two ways. I also had a *funny* feeling I already knew which way it would go!

The deceased man showed me how the nurse's uniform was above the knee, I mean, way above the knee and almost to the buttocks. I thought this cheeky soul was being just a little bit too cheeky. It was another one of those messages I had a distinct feeling I would be getting into trouble with … again! Anyhow, I didn't quite know at the time how I was going to say what I was being shown. Nonetheless, I'd seen it, so I had to say it. "Say what you see," as Roy Walker from Catch Phrase would say.

People in the hall were laughing at me because I was laughing. They didn't even know what I was laughing at. So, I just came out with it and asked, "I've got a gentleman standing with me who wants to have a conversation with a nurse, or the uniform of a nurse. Anyone, please?" It wasn't much to go on, but it was all I had to work on. Still laughing, I put my hand up in front of me making a gesture of 'Stop!' 'Hang on' and said, "I can't be sure if I'm seeing a real nurse, (tongue in cheek) or someone dressed up in one of Ann Summer's nurse's outfits."

Oh! God was I laughing. I couldn't control or compose myself as my laughter got louder and louder. The more I laughed the more people laughed. I grabbed a tissue to wipe my eyes running like a bloody river as tears of laughter ran down my face. I was worried my Itsy and Bitsy lashes would

192

come unstuck and take residence upon my cheeks - or fall to the floor. I had visions of me crawling around on my hands and knees looking for them. I almost lost it for a moment. What do I mean almost? I did lose it! Well, wouldn't you have done too?

I really didn't expect anyone to admit to this message. Mostly because I thought the deceased man was winding me up. Yeah! They do that sometimes. But to my surprise, and probably everybody else's someone did. I could see a lady raising her hand as she jumped up and down in her seat shouting out, "My friend next to me, it's my friend, she was just literally showing me a picture of her at a party in a nurse's uniform - it's on her phone." Now everyone's eyes turned to where the lady was sitting, in the middle row. The entire room was laughing, but I'm not sure whether it was because of the lady ratting out her friend, or because the message was being accepted. I had my suspicions and believed it was the former.

All eyes were on the ladies sitting together, followed by a lot of hesitation and excitement. The lady reached down into her friend's handbag on the floor and fumbled around. After a few seconds she took out her friend's mobile phone. Raising it above her head, she shouted out, "Look!" Having turned a lovely fifty shades of red, the lady's friend looked on as the picture of her in a nurse's uniform was being shown to everyone in the hall. I took that as good validation if ever I needed any. Thankfully, the lady really was amused and enjoyed the connection to the deceased gentleman. I have a smile on my face as I say, "Trust no one!"

Little White Box

Whenever I have to give a message to someone who has lost a baby, it is always incredibly and emotionally difficult. I always feel a lump form in my throat when a baby comes through. I always feel goose bumps forming on my arms, too.

There was a time I didn't want to talk about dead, lost, miscarried, still-born babies because of my own loss. It was a fear I always had in connecting to babies. I just didn't want to do it. Yet, I have to, and I'm obliged to because even the souls of babies have a voice they want to use. Babies want to be heard and I always feel honoured to speak on their behalf. I'm compelled to speak on their behalf. Their own Mother and parents want me to speak on their child's behalf.

I can still feel those goose-bumps when I remember a particular demonstration at a show I was doing. I was choking back tears as I connected to a Mother figure who had stepped forward to visit. I felt a huge sense of sadness with her. She was giving me information connected to names and dates. I asked my audience if anyone could take the information. A young lady didn't hesitate as she raised her hand. She accepted the information being given from the deceased lady standing next to me.

However, I soon understood why I felt an unusual amount of sadness when the deceased lady showed me a *little white box*. She was holding this tiny little box in her arms. The box was in the shape of a coffin. My heart sank - this wasn't good. It meant I would have to acknowledge and talk about the loss of a baby. The coffin lid slid open and I could see the baby lying sweetly and serenely inside. He looked so angelic.

194

As I looked at him, he became aware of me and started to smile and giggle. I could see he was happy. This was the message he wanted me to give to his mother. He was no longer in his coffin, instead he was being looked after by his Grandparent. This was the way his Mother last saw him. This is what he had to show me as evidence.

I could feel the energy drain from me as I prepared myself to deliver this message. Looking at the lady who had raised her hand to connect to this angelic tiny soul I asked, "Darling, I'm so sorry, do you understand a *little white box,* please?" I paused for a moment as I gently asked again, "Do you understand a baby in a *little white box,* please?" I tried to avoid the word coffin as I waited for her response. The young lady immediately knew what I was talking about and broke down crying. I was nervous as I asked her, "Are you OK, darling?" she replied "Yes, I'm sorry." I told her, "Please … don't be sorry. We don't have to do this if you don't want to - I know you have been through a very difficult time, bless you."

There was a moment of silence as I felt the emotions from every single person in that hall. I felt everyone listening to me whilst looking at the young lady I was connecting to. There was so much empathy filling the room. I felt the love coming from everyone's heart. Tears were streaming down the lady's face. I didn't know whether to continue or not. I didn't even know if I could continue. I couldn't begin to feel what she was feeling. Perhaps the loss of her baby was what brought her here, or why would she want to be here? In my heart, I knew she needed to.

After a few minutes of silence, she pleaded with me to continue. I said, "Darling, I'm being shown a card with a blue cot on the front that was given to you. Does this make sense?" She responded, "Yes, it was a card from Mum." I continued speaking softly, "Your baby boy is OK, he is showing himself laughing and giggling. He said he is happy he is being looked after. He said he 'doesn't want you to carry the burden of his loss for the rest of your life.' He said, 'Tell Mum I'm sorry, but she needs to look forward to the future now. I'm still going to be part of her future, tell that to my Mum."

After I finished delivering the message, I could see the lovely lady's face change into one of happiness as she smiled and said, "Thank you." It was like a weight had been lifted off her shoulders. I could only hope it was time for her to close this chapter of sadness that had been affecting her life. She had been given validation of her baby being OK. It was something she needed to hear. I believe she can now be at peace whilst still holding a very special place in her heart for her son. Her baby was being looked after. It was a beautiful bond of love between Mother and Son that will never be broken. I want to thank every single person who helped this Mother get through this conversation. Because of you, I know she felt truly loved and truly at peace. You helped her and her baby son to heal. Thank you.

The 13th

When a client, Loretta, booked a group reading with me there was a change of venue at the very last minute. Loretta's husband had told her she couldn't hold the group psychic night at their home, mostly because he felt a little uncomfortable. Understandable. He didn't know about my work, so I respected and appreciated his concern. It didn't stop Loretta from wanting to go ahead with the booking, she was determined. Fortunately, a friend of hers, Lis, offered to host it at her home instead. Location was not going to be a problem. The night was going to happen for all of us, no matter what.

When I arrived at Lis' house, I could hear the laughter coming from the ladies who had come along to have a conversation with their loved ones. I could also feel a sense of apprehension, nervousness and excitement as I walked through the door. I love receptions like these as it builds the energy I need to work with. There was a lot of giggling ladies I would be working with, I was excited for them. I only hoped they hadn't helped themselves to too much 'Spirit' before I started work!

I slid off my shoes in the hallway tucking them into a corner before I hung up my coat behind a door. Lis directed me into the room where the guests had gathered and were waiting for me. The ladies were busy sorting out their seats and where they were going to sit. Some of them quickly changed their seating plans when I mentioned dead people stood to the right of me. The ladies were eagerly waiting for me to open my door to the Spirit World. They were waiting for me to start the conversations they would be participating in. I was excited for both worlds. I could feel the night was going to be good.

I could feel the energies around me and in the room buzzing. I looked forward to the work ahead, I couldn't wait to start. I felt the room fill up with Spirit and their loved ones who were visiting. They were waiting to have a conversation. There were a few nervous sighs amongst the smiles as I introduced myself and explained how I worked.

Once I got started the lights started to rapidly flicker. There were more nervous sighs, giggles and looks of shock. I reassured everyone that it was a sign Spirit was just as happy as they were to be with us. I didn't want anyone to be, or indeed feel nervous. I didn't want to build a wall between me and the person I was connecting to. If someone put a wall up, then any information given may not be taken because the person would be too scared.

People often ask me if Spirit can follow them home. It's a good question and the answer I give is 'Yes.' Because, technically they can, but only to continue to share their love. It's not unusual either for a person not wanting to connect with me for fear of what I will say in front of their friends. Everyone has a secret to keep from their past. And, with me and my work, it doesn't stay a secret.

However, whenever I work Spirit – Spirit, not me, mostly always save the best till last. So, I had just one more connection to make, and one more conversation to have. It came from a lovely deceased lady, Marianne, who acknowledged having passed with cancer. Her link was to Lis, the house owner. As I told her about Marianne, I mentioned how she was describing the upper part of her body being diseased with cancer before she passed. Lis accepted the information to be correct. Marianne also mentioned how she had recently passed. And, that she had passed on the 13th. Lis also accepted this date of her friends passing to be true. A few of the other ladies could also identify with Marianne as being their friend too. They recalled some of their best memories with her. They validated what Marianne had said in how she lived life to the full. They were happy knowing their friend was no longer suffering and her transition had been a peaceful one. Marianne really was the life and soul of the party. Not only did she come with the beautiful white light, but she also caused the flickering of the lights.

There was certainly a lot of love in the room, and in the house. It was a good house to work in. When the end of the night came, I looked around at each person feeling pleased I had done really well in giving each one of them a message. I gave everyone enough evidence in the memories to heal their hearts and the hearts of those who visited. I gave each lady memories of the messages that were meant to be given to them.

Roots

During a service at a Spiritualist Centre, I was connecting to a lady who I'll refer to as 'Rachel.' Rachel was sat at the back of the hall. She had connected to information relating to her deceased Father. He had stepped forward to visit and have a conversation with his daughter. She smiled at me and acknowledged her Father, and at the same time seemed to be delighted I had chosen her. Although technically, it's not me who picks people to give a message to, it's Spirit.

I found the message and information going so well until he mentioned a name. I called to Rachel asking, "Would you understand the name 'John', please?" She thought for a moment before shaking her head saying, "No, sorry, not for me." I asked the deceased man, "Darling, are you sure about the name, please?" He replied, "Yes, it's John." I looked at Rachel and repeated the name again. But once again, she couldn't accept it. I told her, "Darling, you need to keep searching, keep looking."

Far from thinking I was mad, this didn't make any sense as she continued to shake her head. The name John just couldn't be taken. She spoke softly as she said, "Carole, thank you, I will hold on to the information." I thanked her for the beautiful connection and memories we had shared for those few moments. There was so much evidence Rachel took which all made sense. I had no reason to disbelieve her 'John' because somehow, he would make sense later on.

Weeks later, I served the Spiritual Centre again. As soon as I walked through the door I was greeted by Rachel. She had a big smile on her face as she walked towards me. Excitedly, she started to explain how 'John' was significant to her after all. Apparently, she had been wondering about her ancestry and felt pushed to research her family tree at the library. She was glad she had. It appeared that she uncovered some persons of interest, this alone had astonished her. The information had finally fallen into place for Rachel around the unknown name of 'John.' Rachel told me how she felt she belonged to her family now because of what she found out in the search. She knew and understood more about her family roots. She understood why I had given her the message from her loved one who told her to "Keep searching and keep looking." Which is exactly what she did.

Deceased souls are not supposed to predict, but mine do, and I allow them to because of the relevance. This can prove difficult when I work in Spiritual churches as messages are supposed to be related to evidence of the deceased soul only. Any connection to the future is generally not permitted or accepted because it allegedly does not come from 'Spirit'. Therefore, it is not recognised as evidence. Personally, I believe if evidence has already been given from a deceased soul, any other information given is from Spirit, too. In my view, if a Spirit soul wants to say or show something connected to the future, it should be included within the message.

I don't like to work on church platforms as a norm, because my way of Mediumship just doesn't fit in with the rules and regulations churches endorse. I believe any message given in a Spiritual reading in my understanding should be enjoyed in its entirety, not through nit-picking. I also believe that since this is a 'natural' gift I have developed, we should not be forced to go to church to practice it. It's not something I can honestly say I picked up or learnt from church.

To lead a service on the platform at a Spiritual church or Spiritual Centre is a privilege, and an honour. To be appreciated and respected through the messages that come from both worlds is always a sign of respect to me as a Medium.

Shillings and Pence

During a Skype reading with a client, Sue, I had mentioned the name 'Barry' which she connected to. Sue was looking at me very attentively waiting for more information in the message I was giving her. Barry, a visiting Spirit soul was talking to me non-stop. Seriously, if he had a breath, I would have asked him to take one! No matter, I still love each and every soul who chooses to have a conversation with me.

I listened to the information he was giving before I mentioned to Sue, "Would you understand this gentleman as being quite angry, please?" She laughed as she said, "Yes! He was." Not holding anything back, I told her, "He said to tell you he was a bit of a bastard and would swear a lot." Sue again laughed as she replied "Yes, he was, that was him." Barry talked to me some more and I told Sue, "He said he regretted doing what he did. He said he made a lot of wrong choices. He was sorry you ended up not seeing much of him, and that he left without any explanation. He said he was sorry how he had broken your heart." I continued to ask Sue, "Does all that make sense, please?" Once again, Sue accepted and confirmed the information to be true. Apparently, from what Barry had said he felt he had left his ex-wife in a right mess.

I carried on with Barry's message saying, "He said he wished he could wave a magic wand and change the things that had happened between you." Sue smiled and nodded. I said, "He wants you to know no one can take away the sentiments of your wedding ring." Barry was very chatty, there was so much he wanted to say. He didn't hold back as I said to Sue, "He wants to mention 29th June as being important, and 1988 being significant. Sue

202

replied, "This was the date we moved in together. The year 1988 was when we got married." So many memories Barry wanted to bring back. I continued, "Sue, would you understand the reference to a funfair and candy floss and how it was connected to his name, please?" She replied, "Barry Island, Wales, is where we had taken our son." I was pleased so much information and validation had happened during that message. It didn't end there. I could feel the energy change and another visitor step forward. He too was eager to speak to Sue.

The visitor was another gentleman and as he came close, he said, "Carole, I'm Dad. Tell Sue 13th August is important, please." I said, "Sue, I have another gentleman here for you, darling, who claims to be a Father figure. He is referencing 13th August as important, is that right, please?" Sue replied, "Yes, that's my Dad. It was the date he passed away." I smiled as I looked at Sue saying, "Dad's mentioned there being five brothers. And something about 'shillings and pence." Sue acknowledge the five brothers including himself but the 'shillings and pence' didn't make sense at all. I repeated it again a few more times as I knew it was an important memory. It wasn't long before Sue realised how her Dad was talking about her wooden stool money box. It was a box she had as a child. Written on the box were also the words, 'Our little girl has lots of good sense, she saves in this stool all her *shillings and pence.*'

Sue's Dad continued to talk as I asked, "Would you understand about a unit being built, and how it was all mucked up, and the new windows, please?" Sue confirmed her mum had mucked up the unit and they both had the new windows fitted. Before Sue had finished validating confirmation of her Dad's message, another deceased gentleman stepped forward. As I felt this new energy of another visitor, I asked, "Hello darling, who are you, please?" He replied, "Jim, I'm Jim. December 12th is important, but please mention the letter." I thanked him for the information, as I always do. So, I asked Sue, "Can you connect to December 12th with a deceased gentleman, please?" And, "Oh! he also references a letter?" She nodded accepting the information saying, "Yes, he's my favourite uncle who passed on that date. He also wrote a letter which I still have in my pocket."

There were a good few visitors from Heaven that stepped through to connect to Sue, who was completely overwhelmed, as you can imagine. Sue's family are the ones who brought lots of evidence with their love and memories through Skype to the screen. Memories that made magical moments in both worlds. The next day I received a message from Sue validating in disbelief what I had told her. She couldn't dismiss the information I had given in the messages she had received. Sue clearly had a lot of love that continued to embrace her from her family in the Spirit World.

God Smacked

At my shows, there's no such thing as a lack of evidence. Annmarie came along to one and was in for quite a shock. The evidence she received just kept on coming. After the show, and so she could share her experience with others, she wrote and told me;

"I was attending one of Carole's psychic evenings, which by the way I was reluctant to go to. I always sit on the fence regarding anything psychic. However, I decided to go along to see what it was all about. I was taken back at what came. Carole asked if anyone could take the name 'Bradley'. I have a son called Bradley. I wanted to wait to see if anyone else took the information. No one did, so I raised my hand. Carole connected to me straight away giving me his date of birth. She also said there was another name that was 'Jacob'. I confirmed this to be one of my other son's. I was also given my correct star sign, then the date of 1968, to which I couldn't place at the time. It wasn't until after returning home I realised it was my Grandmother's year of death. Carole had also told me that someone was going to buy a moped, to which of course I didn't take, mostly because I didn't know anyone who was thinking of buying a moped. But when I spoke to my son, he confirmed he was thinking of buying one. I was told by Carole that she was talking to my parents in Spirit and that my Father was saying I had to get my eyes checked. My Dad, he always told me to take my health seriously. I knew this was true as I have a sight problem that will eventually cause loss of sight. I also hadn't been taking my diabetes medication. Carole told me how my Dad said, "F@cking sort it out!" My Dad did swear at me

when he was alive. He was always telling me take my health seriously.
Carole had also said my Mum had come to wish her Grandchildren well.
They were my mum's life, she adored them all. Carole confirmed my Father
had a heart attack a few years before passing, and yes this was also true.
She also reminded me how my Dad used to take me fishing as a child, and
this was true, too. Everything Carole said was exactly correct, and I must
say, I was utterly 'gob smacked' at the evidence. It was an enjoyable
experience and glad I went along."

Chapter 22
Magic Moments & Memories

The Lion, the Shoe and the Attic

Memories are not something that can be erased or easily forgotten, that much we know. I'm pleased that the memories I leave with people are long-lasting. I am pleased to see how the memories through the *visitations and conversations* I give are comforting, healing and of benefit to the people who receive them.

I am always so pleased to see the difference a message can make to people, that's why I've added a few extra memories here. I want to share with you how a message, no matter how long, or how short it is will be important for the person receiving it.

So, bearing in mind the importance of information given and received, I can tell you how Daryl, a friend of mine, was only too pleased to let me know about a message I gave to him. And, as this message showed, sometimes information isn't always for the person receiving it. Here's what Daryl wrote;

"I have known Carole both professionally and as a personal friend now for more than 10 years. Her readings and gentle observations have always been spookily accurate and very revealing. She with her Spiritual friends have guided me with total impartiality to make some very important life-changing decisions – and her advice has always helped me more than I can say in words alone. There is one particular reading that stands out for me. It was

when she asked about 'a lady who gave you furniture'. I instantly knew exactly who she was talking about. Carole was talking about a dear friend, and very much a sceptic when it comes to anything to do with contacting the Other Side. Carole mentioned shoes and a lion. This baffled me as this person is not a shoe person at all, and as for the lion, I didn't think that could be right at all.

Anyway, a few days later I mentioned to this friend of mine what Carole had said. Her jaw dropped. At the time of the reading she was in her attic sorting out old shoes and had come across an old comic she had designed years ago. The comic featured a lion as a central character. As my friend and I were in separate houses in Devon at the time of the reading, and Carole was on the other end of a computer located close to Heathrow Airport, there was no way of rationally explaining that one away as something being made up!"

The Kitten & The Clown

I was demonstrating at a group reading with a few ladies when I connected to Susan. The conversation was going great, until that was at least when I made a reference to clowns. Susan was laughing and nodding as I gave information from her deceased loved one about clowns. She hated clowns. I know the feeling well.

As we were all laughing at this, the little kitten of the house calmly strolled across the room. She sat right in front of me on the spot where I was standing. Without hesitating, she dropped something at my feet before running off. Honestly, I can't tell you how we weren't the only ones having conversations with visitors from the Spirit World. The little kitten was too, apparently. She had carried in her mouth all the way across the room her own little fluffy toy. It was a clown and she had dropped it right on que of my talking about one. How on earth do you explain that? You just don't. It was certainly good validation of what we were talking about. Clever Kitty! Animals really are psychic and really do see the 'dead'.

Reach for the Stars

I was describing a male presence standing beside me at another group reading. He announced himself as 'Tony'. During my conversation with him I could feel my arms drop to my side. I could feel they were heavy. It was a sluggish feeling. I was also describing to the group how I couldn't feel my legs. My legs felt as though they weren't there. At that moment, a young lady, Angie, burst out crying and accepted the information. The person I was describing and having a conversation with was her brother. I gave some dates of birthdays and passing's, all to which was accepted. I told how her brother wanted to remind her of the song made famous by the group, 'S Club 7' - 'Reach for the Stars'.

At first the song didn't make sense to Angie, but then after a few moments she realised just how significant the song was. It was after her brother's passing that Angie had set up a support group in her brother's name aptly called 'Reach for the Stars.' Tony had multiple sclerosis. He wanted to thank his sister for what she had done by setting up a group in his name. For me, this was a privileged conversation with an honourable memory. God Bless, Tony.

Benny and The Jets

I get to hear a lot of songs when I'm working. So, when I was amongst a lot of ladies at one particular group reading I found myself singing. I was attempting to sing along to one of Elton John's songs, 'Benny & The Jets'. Because, the Father of one of the ladies had stepped forward to visit his daughter, Lisa. The lights were flashing consistently and quite erratically as I spoke to Lisa's Dad. I think he really wanted us all to enjoy the party. The light show with the electrics was amazing.

Even though this house wasn't haunted, it would have felt like it. Especially if people were there for any reason other than me being there to demonstrate evidence of the afterlife. Anyway, Lisa looked shocked as she cupped her face with her hands. She was both excited and crying at same time, shouting, "Wow! Wow! Wow!" Followed by, "That's my Dad!" Lisa told how she had been playing the song just last week with her brother. She told how she had asked him if he remembered this song. It was a song their Dad loved. He remembered.

Lisa sent me a message soon after telling me, "It was an amazing night. I felt closer to my Dad than ever since his passing nine years ago. This year, on the anniversary of his death, was the first time I haven't cried due to your lovely messages, so thank you so much." - Lisa. Lisa's Dad would have been proud of her and her brother. He would have been proud of himself, too, for giving such an evidential message to his children.

The House at 54

During a demonstration at a Spiritualist Centre, I was aware of a Spirit lady who stepped forward to have a conversation of her own. Following a few details, a connection was made to her daughter in the audience. Information I was given during our conversation related to a month and date of her partner's birthday. Additionally, I was given the month and date of her brother's birthday, too. Then, just for good measure in our conversation, the number 54 was referred to as a memory link. This turned out to be the door number on the house at 54 where she lived at. Isn't it amazing how our loved ones still visit us and give us evidence of the number on our door? Nothing like having a beautiful feeling in knowing you still have visitors calling on you from Heaven - from people you love!

Sally

During a public demonstration, I was once again made aware of a song behind a memory that would be significant to someone. I found myself having a conversation with a Father figure whose daughter was sat in the audience. She was able to accept him as her Dad following on from the few names I gave. As the conversation between us continued, tears fell from her face when I mentioned how I could hear 'Sally' being sung. I also mentioned how 'Sally' was my very first record sung by Gerry Monroe. It was also a record I bought when I was 11 years old. In fact, it was my first record I purchased.

I waited a while for, Vicky, the lady who's name I got to know, and for her to respond. Unfortunately, she shook her head. She couldn't take it. It didn't make sense to her. I asked her Father for more information, which I got as he said, "Carole, it's Sally down the Alley." I relayed this information back to Vicky. I could now see by the look on her face how meaningful it was. She shouted out, "Yes! it was Robert Palmer's hit song, "Sneaking Sally through the Alley." She also confirmed how this song was a favourite song of her departed Husband, too.

After I had finished demonstrating Vicky came up to me with a big smile on her face. She wanted to show me her play list on her mobile phone. It included her Husband's favourite song that had been mentioned. Her Husband, who was with her Father in the Spirit World, had also stepped forward to join in the conversation during the message. His passing had taken place just six weeks earlier. She was really happy to know how they were both together. Vicky was happy to hear how they shared memories of their favourite song together.

The Letter

Priti, a lady who came to one of my shows sent me feedback after telling me how she had been a member of my audience. She wanted me to know I had picked her out to have a reading. She wrote and told me;

"Not only were the dates and names spot on, but there was one piece of vital information given that was significant and relevant'.

In her feedback she reminded me how I had asked during her message if she knew why a 'certain person' would be continually opening an envelope and taking out a letter, reading it and placing it back inside the envelope again? The lady wanted to confirm this information as true and further explained:

"I had sent a letter just two weeks earlier, on the 15th November (which was the date you had given) to a previous long-term acquaintance. The letter simply had one line saying, 'Happy Birthday'. I was grateful to hear this as it gave me confirmation the right person had received it and was still thinking about me. No other person was aware that I had sent a disguised envelope, so it was astonishing to hear it come out. There was other information given about this individual which also proved to be correct. I am so grateful I went, but I was so happy Carole connected to me."

Emotional Moment

When Spirit share an abundance of love through their conversation, I know I am doing something right. So, when Kosola, a lovely man, came to see me, he didn't just visit me the once. He came back time and time again after his first visit. He was also willing to travel the long distance it took too. When I asked Kosola if he had a memory of a reading with me, he wrote;

"I was told about Carole from a friend of mine. My friend thought due to my own personal circumstances a visit would help me. I went in cold not knowing what to expect. I was a little anxious and whole lot nervous. I got a lot more than what I bargained for. I certainly was not ready for one of the most emotional moments in my life, where years of tension held on my shoulders were finally released!

At the time of writing this, I have been to see Carole on three occasions, and the reason I return is because of the comfort and love I feel. I feel comforted from the connections from the Other Side encouraging me. And ultimately, the clarity and confirmation that all will be well. As well as the accuracy of my situations and future, it's a phenomenal experience for anyone who is willing to believe and looking for something to be answered. The experience is full of love, it's personal and thoughtful.

I was very lucky to get messages from my Grandmother who is looking over me and my family. The whole experience has given me strength and confidence, as well as a sense of peace and tranquillity. Everything that my mind has been looking for. As well as the tears, there was laughter, but above all a feeling of love and warmth. Thank you for your time, Carole, and understanding me. It was an extremely Spiritual and calming experience that I would recommend to anyone."

Quirky

Sometimes, I don't realise how I stare at people. Sometimes, I know it's not even me starring at people, but Spirit themselves looking through my eyes. I only became aware of this through Natalie, an academic, who had contacted me after reading my book. Here's what Natalie wrote;

"Hi Carole, I have finished reading your book and would like to congratulate you on the journey you have taken me, and I am sure other readers on. I thought the book was very 'you'. The book, "The Living Spirit, One Woman's Battle Amongst Ghosts, Spirits and The Living', was filled with your personality and energy. Sometimes I felt you were speaking to me through your little quirky phrases, phrases I remembered when we saw each other regularly in the Graduate school. I think you cleared up many questions I have had in my mind about you. So, thank you for opening up your soul to others and so to me. I now understand the reason you used to throw insignificant numbers at me whenever we met. I understand the reason for your intense eye contact with me whenever we used to meet. I also understand why I have kept my distance from you – not because you were scary but because I was unwilling to face myself through you. I loved the way you talked about the art deco on your pillow and the way you will tell your ghosts to 'get lost', and the way you referred to your Husband as 'the Hubby.' This all made you so real and endearing but most importantly, it validated your stories which I found terribly captivating. I loved your honesty and your intensity. The book was a truly captivating one, which took me two days to read because I could not put it down. Thank you, and, I don't ever say this

to anyone - but feel comfortable in saying to you. God Bless you"

A Few Home Truths

I met Adrian at a Healing Centre. After a Skype reading with him, this is what he wrote;

"Carole is an amazing Medium I've known for some time and it's always a pleasure to speak with her, and even more special when I book to have a reading with her. Carole's connections and conversations with those on the Other Side is amazing. She is able to describe with incredible accuracy who she is working with. Carole has confidently named a number of members of my family who have passed (whom she had no prior knowledge of), how they look, their mood and the information they wished to convey.

Carole is a 'professional' in the greatest sense of the word. She works in an incredible manner to deliver the messages with detail, clarity and compassion and to leave you in no doubt as to whom the information is from and for. Carole's integrity is impeccable, particularly when Spirit needs to deliver a few 'home truths' that may be hard to take, but necessary to be said none the less! Her readings always give me food for thought and I love that about the way Carole works. Spirit are not afraid to give her difficult, sometimes complex things to portray as they know she is more than capable of interpreting and portraying them with great accuracy, gravitas and always balanced with the right level of compassion. The depth and richness of the information you receive makes a reading with Carole a very personal experience and her abilities are something very rare and special in a Medium. Booking a reading with Carole is something to be cherished and treasured."

Good Advice

Kelly, who is a Facebook friend of mine lives in the USA. When she wrote asking for advice, I gave it through Skype during a reading. It was shortly after Kelly wrote and told me of her journey she had through my reading. Here's what she wrote;

"Carole, I wanted to let you know that today, all my test results came in 'All clear'. I cannot express to you how your words and advice changed not only my thoughts, but how I reacted to this whole situation. I think until someone goes through something scary, one never knows, but I know this – your advice, you're calming words, guidance, prayers and good thoughts completely transformed not only this experience, but my way of thinking. I know that you said it was always in me, but you taught me how to focus and create the change that I needed. I know in my heart it would not have been like this. I amaze myself! This skill is something that I know I will use over and over. And I know that I will be very blessed to be able to pass along to others who need it and proudly tell them who taught me. I had to let you know what a blessing and a gift you are, and how much I truly appreciate just you, being you, and how thankful I am. But for anyone who does not know, trust me, Mrs. Bromley knows of what she speaks. And I, for one, am very grateful. On the day of my visit to the hospital I actually sat and read your words while I was waiting to be called in. As I had read them again the night before, it was simply amazing the calming effect. And I also wanted to touch base and thank you for your calming words."

In giving you an update; Kelly wrote to me again to tell me how her doctor doing the procedure actually commented on how calm she was and that she was the calmest person he has ever had in there. She had told him how 'she was not alone in the room and that she had 'Spirits' with her.' She was happy as she told me how her doctor had smiled at her and patted her hand.

Kelly further wrote;

"I did as you said and welcomed the test and asked my Spirit Guide for comfort and my Angel to be with me."

Kelly told how my words had helped to turn her thoughts around, saying:

"The entire test was virtually pain free. I felt no injections, stinging from anaesthetic, nothing that the doctor said I would."

Kelly didn't stop there, either, and went on to write;

"I truly felt so relaxed that I thought they had turned the light off; I could have taken a nap. I also know that whatever comes I have the calm and strength to face it. Thank you."

Kelly told me how she was no longer fearful because she had welcomed the knowledge I had given. She expressed how she could not take any action if she was unaware and wrote;

"I cannot thank you enough, Carole, for your kind words and wonderful

advice. The peace of mind I feel is amazing and I credit you with a very large part of it, you are a blessing to all of us."

I Can't Get No Satisfaction

There are no limits as to where or how Spirit will communicate. So, when I did a reading for Randy, a lady in Texas via Skype, I was pleased to hear from her just how she felt it went. She wrote;

"My Dear Carole, I can't thank you enough for the time and help you gave me. I was so tickled with my sister I was dancing around the bathroom singing, "I can't get no satisfaction!" I e-mailed my niece and shared her mom's joy with her. And, by the way, the way you helped me resolve the issues with my mom - I just can't help but cry for the peace and love that came through for us both.

You! You are my go-to psychic and always will be. You have healed me and given me gifts of happiness and joy that I can never repay. I knew you were put in my path for a reason and I am so happy to know you. I also want to thank you for the reading you gave my Brother. My Brother was blown away when his wife came through; he questioned her place on the Other Side because she took her life. He is so grateful to know she's happy and watching over him and their girls. He was also overjoyed to hear from our Mother, and we were both surprised to hear she'd been hanging out with us. He is a true believer because of you."

Native Language

It doesn't matter what language you speak, Spirit will always translate it into my language, English. When a client, Deanna, came to me for a reading she was surprised I could translate the evidence given during our conversation with her Grandparents, especially since they never spoke a word of English, themselves. Here's what Deanna wrote;

"Thank you for the reading Carole ... I'm still crying! I was so happy to hear the messages of love and support from my late Dad and Grandparents... and laughing at the same time, hearing you speak in a different language (my Grandparents' native, but completely alien to you), or at least attempting to pronounce the words. It was certainly an experience I will never forget ... so, so overwhelmed."

Reaching Out

Spirit can connect anytime, anywhere in the world. Another client of mine, Jacquie, who through her reading and having a conversation with her Mother, was also able to connect to her living Brother. Here's what Jacqui wrote;

"Carole, I want to let you know that your connection with my mum had us both laughing, which, of course, is priceless. She was able to tell you who she was and dates that were important, as well as dates that <u>will</u> be important. Her wish for me was that I connect with my Brother. So, I called him after our meeting and we will be having dinner in a few days. The tears I shed were of joy as knowing my Mother is content. And, in her true fashion, was able to tell me to keep my chin up. This ability to connect with her personality was wonderful; the dates you mentioned on changes in my life were right on. Carole, you have been able to help my Mother and I reach out to each other, and this day went by with a feeling of elation. Thank you from the bottom of my heart."

The Messenger

Loved ones will make sure any message they have for someone will get to their 'someone.' During a reading for a client, Carrie, on Skype, she was able to pass the message along to the person it was meant for. Here's what she wrote;

"I had a reading with this wonderful lady. Not only did Carole add pieces to a puzzle I've been trying to find the truth to for the last ten years, but I have looked into what I have been told by Carole and found out so much more. Things I thought had happened haven't, and all sorts of other stuff. I can't thank you enough for the time you spent helping me and my lovely friend in Spirit whom I miss so much. Without you're reading, I would have not known what I do now, and to have passed on what I learned from you to the person that I feel the message was for. So, thank you again."

A Wonderful Gift

The dates and evidence in David's message kept on flowing to give hit after hit after hit. Here's what he wrote;

"Hi Carole, I just want to thank you for the recent reading I had with you. The accuracy within the reading was, quite frankly, astonishing. Certain aspects of the reading I had no knowledge of, but after checking with family members, proved to be correct. Also, you gave me certain dates that were very significant. Throughout the reading I felt completely at ease and enjoyed your warm, friendly and compassionate nature, particularly when you hit on certain personal aspects of my life that only I know of. I have had readings before with other Mediums but can honestly say yours has been easily the best in terms of the delivery, specific information, and overall content. Keep up the good work, Carole, you have a wonderful gift and very strong link with the Spirit World, that time and time again prove there is a life beyond this one."

Somewhere Over The Rainbow

When Monika came to me for a private reading, she never knew just how significant a song would be. Here's what she wrote;

"During my reading with Carole, there was a song she mentioned, 'Somewhere Over the Rainbow', that she claimed was significant. It wasn't at the time, but I found out a few days later my niece auditioned for a part and was going to sing this specific song, only to change her mind and sing something else. Consequently, she didn't pass the audition. She also mentioned a very 'freaky' ex of mine whom I hadn't seen for some time, only to have him text me twenty minutes after leaving Carole's house! It was also mentioned I would have a new job, which I now have so that was spot on, too. Thank you."

The 18th

A student, Sunitta, popped in to see me for a reading one day and afterwards found out some interesting information. Here's what she wrote;

"Hi Carole, many thanks again for the reading session, it has been very helpful and has calmed me down a lot. A few interesting points that have come out. I spoke to my Dad to find out about the number eighteen that you had mentioned relating to a guardian Spirit around me. The eighteenth November is the date my Grandmother died. All the astrologers my parents have consulted in India in the last one year have indicated exactly the same as you. Your reading affirmed a lot of their observations as regards to the nature of the girl and the nature of their marriage. It almost mirrors what they have said. I actually found this quite astonishing given that we come from completely different cultural backgrounds. All of the astrologers we had consulted back home had said that the marriage is going to take place regardless of our efforts to see it not happen. We cannot stop it from happening, you confirmed this. I have also started to focus back on my PhD and set new deadlines to finish the first draft by April, so April also became quite significant to me when you mentioned it." Thank you.

On-Line Chat

Sometimes, we can be in the right place at the right time for a reason. I'm glad I was in my chatroom on my website when I was. There were just two of us, me and Lolly. As I struck up a conversation with Lolly, I became aware of a Father figure from the Spirit World standing by my side. He was Lolly's Grandfather. He also wanted to be part of our conversation. Lolly wrote to me saying;

"Dear Carole, I took my Granddad's death badly and felt guilty for not being at his side. I was so depressed I was suicidal. Then something, or someone, said to go on the internet. Well, I was nervous, but I found my lifesaver in you, Carole. I went to your website and a chat room you had. I hadn't been there long before you picked up on my heart and how I was feeling. I can tell you - you could have knocked me down with a feather. You told me how I took my Granddad to the beach, with Granddad sitting in his navy blazer. But the thing that made me start believing is you Carole is when you told me about my Granddad's eyes and smile. Everyone who knew him loved his smile. Carole, you told me Granddad didn't want me there when he died, as I would have hurt even more. I can honestly say thank you, Carole, for saving my life and for thirteen wonderful years for being my friend, it's an honour."

Without a Doubt

I never know how a reading will go, so when I did a reading for Lesley-Anne, who herself had seen many Mediums before, there was no pressure. Here is what she wrote;

"I cannot thank Carole enough for the reading I had with her. Firstly, let me say that I'd previously seen a number of Mediums/Spiritualists, but they only ever gave me a vague reading, which included Tarot cards. Carole completely gave herself, sympathy and time for which I am eternally grateful. I didn't know her and when we arranged to meet, she didn't want any details of the person that I most wanted to connect with.

Carole welcomed me into her home and in a very relaxing manner, explained that I could write notes throughout and ask questions if I needed. Immediately, she felt that her head hurt and was in pain; until I said that was how my best friend died (of a massive brain haemorrhage) which then stopped the pain, as this was validation. After that, so many details came through that this could only be my dearest best friend, Debbie, who left this world 18th March 2012.

There were many tears from me and some laughter as we shared stories about the significance of the messages coming through. I was amazed, not because I doubted that Carole would do a good reading, but the quality and detail of the reading just blew me away. She has an absolute gift that she is happy to share, and she does so with such flair and style ... a real lady. It's a strange and comforting experience to know that those we love are not lost to us. Carole was able to assure me that there is, without any doubt, more to come after this life on Earth."

Chapter 23
Predictions

Socks

There are a few predictions I want to mention here and thank those who gave me the feedback.

When Siobhan came to see me for a private reading, she had no expectations as to what would happen. What did happen was her Mother came through and started a conversation. As I connected to Siobhan's mum, I was given months and dates that all made sense and were accepted. Then, her Mother started talking about a pair of socks. As I told Siobhan about the sock's she burst out laughing. She looked at me in disbelief that I would mention them. She said she had been thinking about the socks during the drive over to me.

Apparently, it was only family and a close friend who knew how significant the socks were. It was Siobhan herself who had noticed two days before her mother passed that her right sock was inside out. Her Mother told her she couldn't be bothered to change it. Sadly, a few days later Siobhan's mum passed away. The funeral directors had asked Siobhan if there any special requirements for her mum. There was, she asked for the right sock to be inside out because she knew how her Mother would laugh about it. When Siobhan texted me to give feedback on her reading, she told how very happy she was in just hearing about the socks.

There was also an ice rink that was mentioned during the reading that would prove to be important, which at the time I remember Siobhan shaking her head as she told me, "No, that doesn't make sense." I said, "OK, darling, but please keep hold of this information because it will." Siobhan was happy to make a note but really didn't connect to an ice rink.

Siobhan's Mother was doing really well giving a lot of information during her conversation. Information that included details about a nephew's funeral only family knew about. Siobhan's Mother had also been hanging out with her at work. She mentioned how a lady she worked with, whose name I accurately gave, would approach her to make her an offer for something. Again, she dismissed this as she didn't have much to do with the lady.

Just three days later, Siobhan sent me another text confirming an ice rink was being talked about and that it may be installed at or near her place of work. And, she confirmed the lady I had named she worked with had made her an offer to do something together.

Lipstick

I have a lovely Mother, Kay, and daughter, Sophia, who come to see me often in the hope of speaking with their Son and Brother, Andy. He had never let them down at previous appointments and always most certainly makes an appearance as soon as they arrive.

I had the pleasure to meet Andy on one occasion to give him Reiki. Sadly, he was in advanced stages of cancer. The healing wouldn't cure him, but it did give him comfort. He knew too how he would be in good company when he reached Heaven. His own Nan was a Spiritualist, she would also be looking after him on his arrival. He believed in an afterlife. This belief helped him with the strength he needed to face what was to come.

During one of Andy's last conversations with his Sister and Mum, he mentioned how his Mother's Granddaughter, his niece, would sign up for a college course. He also mentioned how she would even wear lots of layers of lipstick. The college they could take, but the lipstick not. The Granddaughter never wore lipstick, nor had she purchased any. It was something she just simply wouldn't do.

The day after the reading I received a text from Sophia saying how surprised her and her mother were as the Granddaughter had signed up for a college course. She had also been out shopping and bought loads of lipstick, which was quite unusual for her!

Due Date

I love being the bearer of good news - especially when it's Baby news! Stacy, a client came for a reading and got a little bit more information than she may have liked. Fortunately, the conversation and information that came from her dear departed Grandad was spot on. Stacy wrote;

"Dear Carole, thank you for the lovely messages that you have brought to us. It all began on Friday, 6th October at a Spiritualist Centre in High Wycombe, Bucks. Dates were given by yourself which mostly we could take, apart from 23rd June. The description you gave of my Granddad was spot on. When I accepted the information, you began working with me. The main part of the message was where you asked me if I was excepting a baby, my reply was, "No", as at this point, I had no idea. You said I was either pregnant at this point or it was going to happen very soon.

A few weeks after receiving the message from you I had all the signs of being pregnant so had done the test. I was, in fact, pregnant! Booking all the appointments with the midwife, I was in fact given the due date of 23rd June, the date that you had told me to keep in my mind as meaning something to me. This was then confirmed on the dating scan at 12 weeks with the due date not changing. However, I have to say, getting to know you were doing a special show at a local Hall in High Wycombe on Friday 13th April, we thought we would be unable to attend. Fate was on our side and the work we had was cancelled. There was only one place we were meant to be. Again, our loved ones love you as much as we do, and the dates came flowing with descriptions. Spot on again. My Granddad along with my Nan *came through you. Part of the message was that there were two birthdays in May - one which is my Granddad's. But, at the moment, we cannot say there are two so watch this space to see if the baby makes an appearance in May or due date in June."*

Chapter 24
Science v Psychic Functioning

Psychic functioning was demonstrated in the project, code-named 'Stargate', started by the U.S. Defence Intelligence Agency (DIA) in 1970, after they believed the Russians were spending 60 million rubles running their own psychotronic research into psychic spying. This programme was subsequently transferred to the Central Intelligence Agency (CIA), which in 1972 was further transferred to and funded by the Stanford Research Institute (SRI), Menlo Park, California.

It was interesting to see how the very fact that both the Russians and Americans invested a huge amount of serious money in such projects. This is an indication of how they perceived there must be something worth financing. Psychics and psychic functioning are a built-in system we all own and can invest in, despite it being usually dismissed out of hand, just because scientists can't find a logical explanation.

However, with so many planets being discovered, it would be such a huge achievement if the Spirit World was also scientifically discovered. As it is, scientists will write about Mediums, the Paranormal and this Other World - The Spirit World - yet, they will do so with a different view. Their own view. In my view, no one can simply write about something that has not been a personal experience, FACT. But … and a BIG butt! … just because something has been academically written about, it is expected other people who are none the wiser will believe in what they are reading. So, can scientists really write factually about other people's paranormal experiences if they have not experienced them first-hand? Call me 'Cranky' but I may just have something here!

We live in a society where no one really knows who to believe let alone what to believe. Some will believe scientists must be right because they have a degree. Whilst others may perhaps believe the word of someone like me, a Medium. Of course, people believe in their own experiences which will perhaps support much of their own paranormal and Spiritual experiences.

Scientific researchers have also led us to believe those with 'psychic functioning' are nothing more than 'nut cases'. Oh dear! This is because they believe there is a 'chemical imbalance' within the brain'. In that case, the good news for most of us, I guess, is there's an awful lot of people out there in the world going nuts with this 'chemical imbalance'. So, if you are one of these people, you'll be happy to know you're not alone!

There is a huge population of people with psychic functioning and Mediumship abilities who cannot possibly all be scientifically examined. For a start, there wouldn't be enough funding. Besides, many people have, or will have, their own psychic, spiritual, or paranormal experience at some point. Not everyone can be examined. But, I do know, and I'm sure you know, too, that it is something we are going to have to live with. Those with psychic functioning are people we are all going to have to live with.

I'd have to seriously ask the question; "Can all these people with psychic functioning seriously be diagnosed with a brain malfunction?" And, "Are we all being wrongly labelled as crazy?" Should we worry? It seems this 'chemical imbalance' is a theory provided by researchers every time a logical explanation cannot be found. Dismissing it is far easier. This unexplained scientific theory has never been questioned, has it?

Don't get me wrong, I have nothing whatsoever against scientists, or scientific research. Quite the opposite. I would love their support in this subject. I would love them to find something that would help me understand just how this gift I have works. Nonetheless, I can't help feeling the wool is being pulled over our eyes with this subject. We have to understand how Spirit, as an energy form, isn't easy to experiment with. Instead, it is best to understand it as an energy when it has been experienced.

Nonetheless, since so many people apparently have this 'chemical imbalance', surely, it is something we should take an interest in, and perhaps ask scientists to prove this theory? Who knows! I do tend to get these crazy thoughts at times.

Some scientists are thankfully and belatedly coming around to this understanding of our Spirit World. One of these scientists, whom I have no connection to whatsoever, is Dr Robert Lanza, a leading expert in Advanced Cell Technology. Dr Lanza published "Biocentrism: How Life and Consciousness Are the Keys to Understanding the Nature of the Universe" (2010).

The conscious mind has the ability to learn many new things as it is forever evolving. Within this evolvement includes psychic functioning and communicating with Spirit souls which are all part of an expanded shared consciousness. Dr Robert Lanza makes an interesting read. His methodology teaches a new theory through the survival of consciousness in *biocentrism,* and where he describes his belief of multiple universes. He includes a theory whereby the body can be dead in one universe whilst the consciousness continues to exist in another.

Naturally, it is a great discovery and one I am not going to argue with. This theory is about the nearest logical `scientific` explanation that I have come across to date. It is one that is of significant value, and of interest to the people of the paranormal world. Perhaps now is a good time to mention how we should all be keeping an 'open-mind' on this subject.

Of course, I don't expect anyone to believe in my world, or begin to understand it. It is something that needs to be experienced for what it is. I believe that alone is a fair comment and a fair view. All I know is that it exists and surrounds us all within a continually expanding quadrant. And because you have purchased my book and are reading it, I know you have an interest, too, in the same belief system as me. I know too, that you wouldn't spend time reading my book if you weren't just a little bit curious of my world.

Glossary

Psychic

A psychic is a person who claims to use extrasensory perception (ESP) to identify information hidden from the normal senses, particularly involving telepathy or clairvoyance, or who performs acts that are apparently inexplicable by natural laws.

Medium

A Medium is a person who has an ability and a gift to interpret information from deceased souls.

Soul

A Soul represents the whole being of a person whether physical and alive, or dead and co-existing in the Spirit World.

Spirit

A spirit is a supernatural entity or being and is representative of a deceased person, ghost, fairy, angel or other entity. A Spirit is often referred to as the consciousness or personality.

Spirit of The Glass

A form of communicating with the dead by using a glass placed in the middle of a table and pieces of paper or cards placed around the glass with letters of the alphabet.

Spirit World

This is a non-physical realm where upon disembodied spirits exist.

Transfiguration

A complete change or form of appearance when a spirit entity masks over a person's facial features.

Trance

Trance is a state of consciousness used by mediums during spiritual communication. The spirit entity will use the mind of the medium to influence its thoughts and emotions.

References

Dr Lanza published "Biocentrism: How Life and Consciousness Are the Keys to Understanding the Nature of the Universe" (2010).

www.carolebromley.com

Printed in Great Britain
by Amazon